Street by Street

OXFORD

ABINGDON, EYNSHAM, KIDLINGTON, WHEATLEY

Appleford, Appleton, Botley, Garsington, Kennington, Long Hanborough, Radley, Sandleigh, Stanton St John, Woodstock, Yarnton

Reprinted August 2003
Ist edition May 2001

© Automobile.Association Developments
Limited 2001

Ordnance Survey® This product includes map data licensed from Ordnance Survey ® with the permission of the Controller of Her Majesty's Stationery Office. © Crown copyright 2003. All rights reserved. Licence number 399221.

Published by AA Publishing (a trading name of Automobile Association Developments Limited, whose registered office is Millstream, Maidenhead Road, Windsor, Berkshire SL4 5GD. Registered number 1878835).

Mapping produced by the Cartographic Department of The Automobile Association. (A01938)

A CIP Catalogue record for this book is available from the British Library.

Printed by GRAFIASA S.A., Porto, Portugal

The contents of this atlas are believed to be correct at the time of the latest revision. However, the publishers cannot be held responsible for loss occasioned to any person acting or refraining from action as a result of any material in this atlas, nor for any errors, omissions or changes in such material. The publishers would welcome information to correct any errors or omissions and to keep this atlas up to date. Please write to Publishing, The Automobile Association, Fanum House, Basing View, Basingstoke, Hampshire, RG21 4EA.

Ref: ML093

Key to map pages	ii-iii
Key to map symbols	iv-1
Enlarged scale pages	2-3
Street by Street	4-81
Index – towns & villages	82
Index – streets	83-90
Index – featured places	90-92

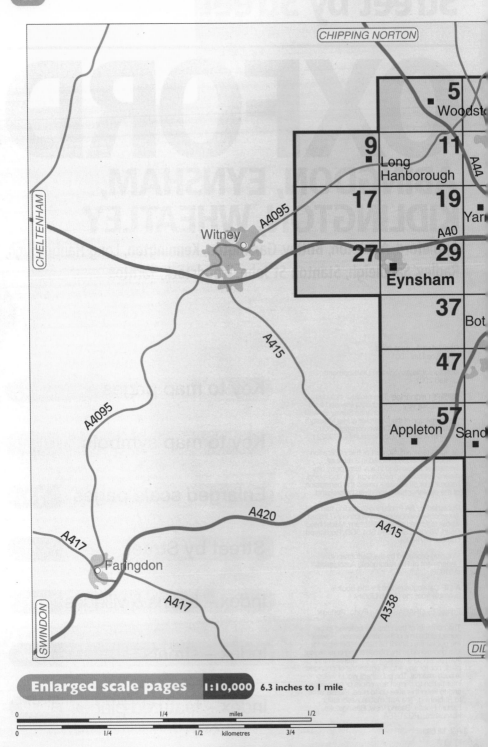

CHIPPING NORTON

5 Woodsto

9 Long Hanborough **11** A44

17 **19** Yar

A4095 A40

Witney **27** **29** Eynsham

CHELTENHAM

37 Bot

A415 **47**

A4095 **57** Appleton Sand

A420 A415

A417 Faringdon

SWINDON A417 A338 DID

Enlarged scale pages 1:10,000 6.3 inches to 1 mile

| 0 | 1/4 | miles | 1/2 |
| 0 | 1/4 | 1/2 kilometres | 3/4 | 1 |

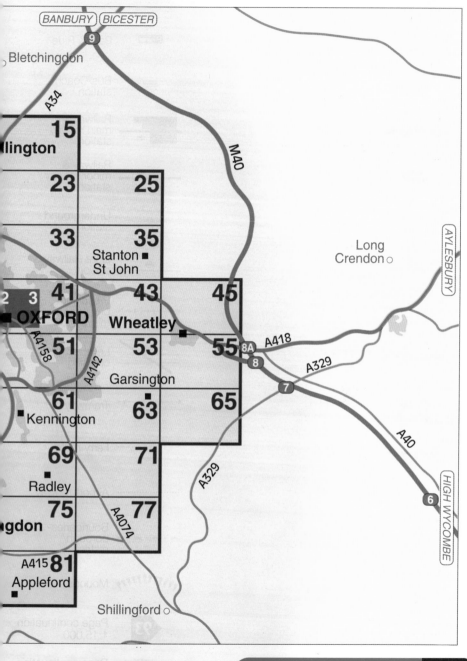

BANBURY BICESTER
9
Bletchingdon

A34

15
llington

23 25

33 35
Stanton ■
St John

Long
Crendon ○

AYLESBURY

M40

41 43 45
■ OXFORD Wheatley ■

A4158
A4142

51 53 55 8A
A418
8

A329

65
63

7

Garsington

61
■ Kennington

A40

69 71
■ Radley

A4074
A329

75 77
gdon

HIGH WYCOMBE
6

A415 81
Appleford
■

Shillingford ○

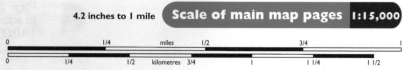

Junction 9	Motorway & junction
Services	Motorway service area
	Primary road single/dual carriageway
Services	Primary road service area
	A road single/dual carriageway
	B road single/dual carriageway
	Other road single/dual carriageway
	Restricted road
	Private road
← ←	One way street
	Pedestrian street
	Track/footpath
	Road under construction
	Road tunnel
P	Parking

P+	Park & Ride
	Bus/Coach station
	Railway & main railway station
	Railway & minor railway station
	Underground station
	Light Railway & station
+++++++	Preserved private railway
LC	Level crossing
•—•—•—•	Tramway
– – – – –	Ferry route
············	Airport runway
– · – · – · –	Boundaries-borough/district
ʌʌʌʌʌʌʌ	Mounds
93	Page continuation 1:15,000
7	Page continuation to enlarged scale 1:10,000

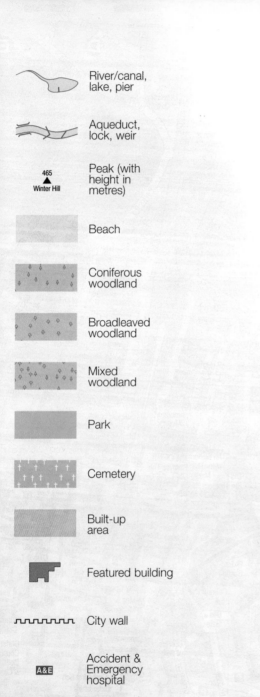

River/canal, lake, pier

Aqueduct, lock, weir

465 ▲ Winter Hill — Peak (with height in metres)

Beach

Coniferous woodland

Broadleaved woodland

Mixed woodland

Park

Cemetery

Built-up area

Featured building

City wall

A&E — Accident & Emergency hospital

Toilet

Toilet with disabled facilities

Petrol station

PH — Public house

PO — Post Office

Public library

i — Tourist Information Centre

Castle

Historic house/ building

Wakehurst Place NT — National Trust property

M — Museum/ art gallery

Church/chapel

Country park

Theatre/ performing arts

Cinema

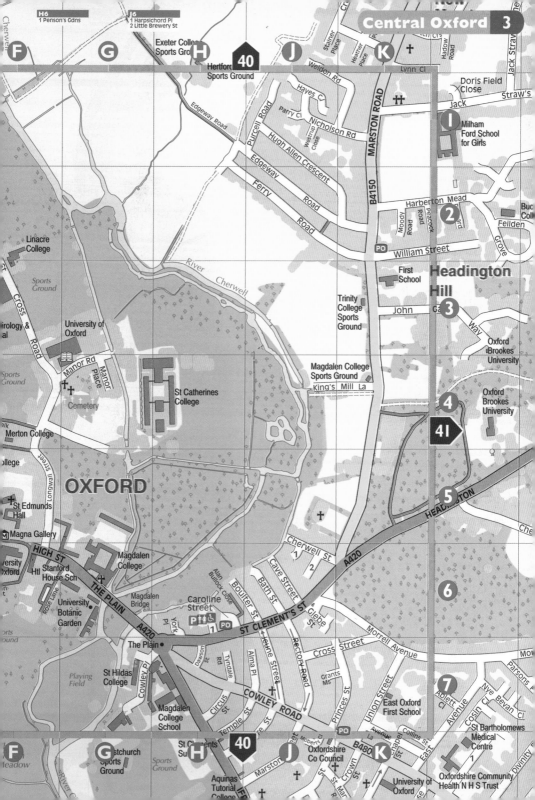

Field
Barn

A

B

C

D

I

Old
Woods

A44

MANOR ROAD

Hill Rise

Vanbrugh
Cl

Rosamund Dr

1

Manor Cl

Westland
Wy

2

Great Park

Column of
Victory

THE CAUSEWA

Park
Farm

Oxfordshire County
Museum

2
Park

Recc

3

Queen
Pool

Grand
Bridge

4

Blenheim
Palace

The
Lake

5

East
End

A

High
Lodge

B

10

C

D

Lane

River Clyne

1 grid square represents 500 metres

E3
1 Upper Brook Hl

F3
1 Campbells Cl
2 Meadow Wk

E F G H

I

River Glyne

Green Lane

Cemetery

Shipton Sla
Farm

2

Glyme Close

Hill

Bear Close

Cem

Kenwood Close

Churchill Cl

Banbury Road

Budds Cl

Hensington

Hensington Close

Marlborough School

Woodstock Swimming Pool

3

6

Upper Ca
Farm

Bear Cl

Union St

Hensington Road

New Road

Boundary

Recreation Rd

Woodstock C of E Primary School

1

Plane Tree Wk

Thicket

Flemings Road

Shipton Road

WOODSTOCK

tors
gery

Cadogan Park

The Ley

Park Side

Princes Ride

Glovers Cl

Briar

2

Hedge End

Crecy

The Covert

Churchill Cl

CAMPSF

4

OXFORD ROAD

A44

UPPER

A4095

Lower Park

5

BLADON ROAD

Orchard Field Lane

WOODSTOCK ROAD

E F H G H

The Homestead

GROVE ROAD

Park Lane

Wolsey Court

6

A B C D Gibraltar

River Cherwell

Oxford Canal Walk

Bunkers Hill

1

BUNKERS HILL

BANBURY ROAD

A4095

Shipton Slade Farm

2

Shipton-on-Cherwell

Jerome Way

ROAD

Birchwood Dr

3

5

CAMPSFIELD

Upper Campsfield Farm

Shipton House

4

BANBURY ROAD

PPER

Canal Road

A4260

Thrupp

5

12

A B C D

Oxford (Kidlington) Airport

1 grid square represents 500 metres

H I
1 Annesley Cl

E   F   G   H

B4027

Bletchingdon
Park

Greenhill
Farm

STATION ROAD

Causeway

Valentia Cl

Coghill

St Giles

PO

1

Lenthal

Oxford Road

Islip Road

I

Bletchingdon Paroc
Controlled Primary

Bletchin

2   B4

3

Canal

nal Wk

Walnut Tree
Cottage

4

**Hampton
Gay**

River Cherwell

Bletchingdon Road

5

Church Lane

Manor
Farm

E   F   I3   G   H

**Hampton
Poyle**

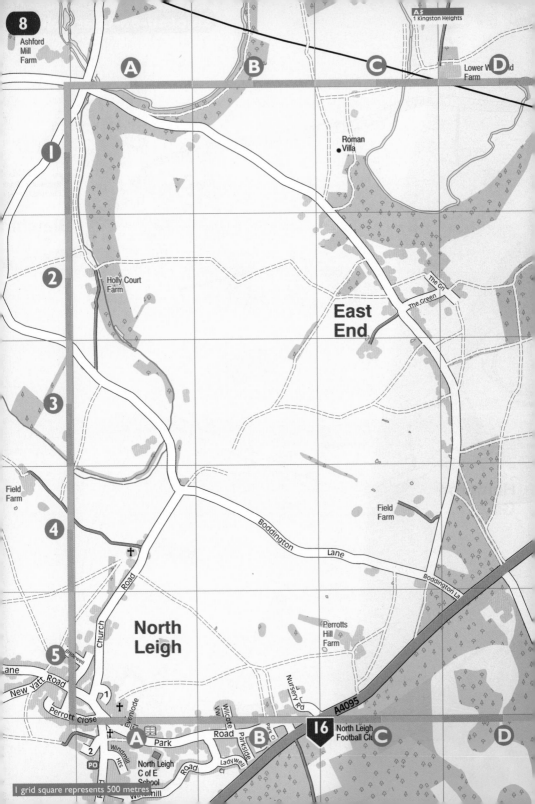

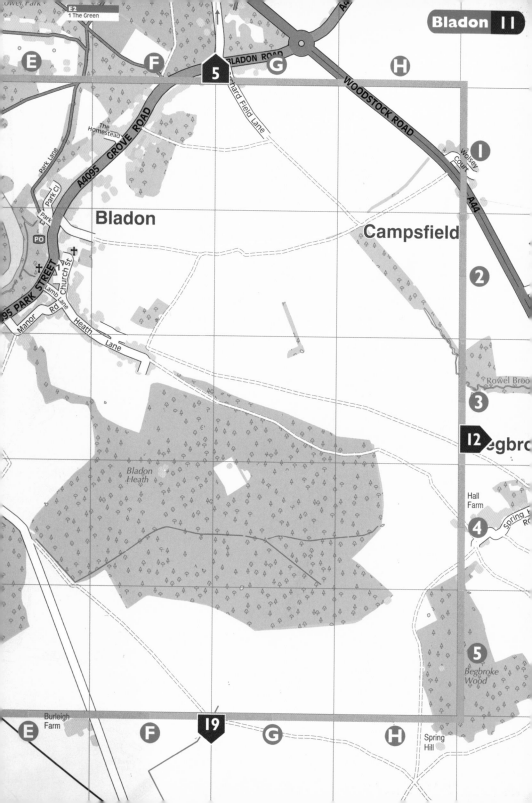

ower Park

E2
1 The Green

BLADON ROAD

5

WOODSTOCK ROAD

A44

E

F

G

H

I

Orchard Field Lane

GROVE ROAD

A4095

Park Lane

Park Cl

Park La

The Homestead

Bladon

Campsfield

PO

Church St

Lamb Lane

95 PARK STREET

Manor Rd

Heath Lane

Wolsey Court

2

Rowel Broo

3

12 egbrc

Bladon Heath

Hall Farm

Spring Rd

4

5

Begbroke Wood

Burleigh Farm

E

F

19

G

H

Spring Hill

Hampton Poyle

KIDLINGTON

Gosford

Manor Farm

Church Lane

River Cherwell

The Moors

The Moorlands

E3
1 Heyford Mead
2 Roundham Cl
3 Wilsdon Wy

E4
1 Belgrove Cl
2 Bellenger Wy
3 Bowerman Cl
4 Fernhill Cl
5 Grovelands
6 The Homestead
7 Morrell Cl
8 Ploughley Cl
9 The Rookery
10 Scott Cl

F3
1 The Closes
2 Curtis Rd
3 Deaufort Cl

F5
1 Cherry Cl
2 Hawthorn Wy
3 Lincraft Cl
4 Magnolia Cl
5 Winston Cl

G3
1 Brasenose Dr

G5
1 Poplar Cl

BANBURY ROAD

A4260

OXFORD ROAD

Bletchingdon Rd

Mill Street

Church Street

Blecheter Rd

Bicester Road

Cherwell Avenue

Watermead

Mill End

Eaton Lane

Water

Cromwell Way

Queens Avenue

Kings Way

Waverley Avenue

Bicester Rd

Edinburgh Drive

Lovelace Drive

Springfield

Evans Lane

Croft Av

Oak Drive

Field Cl

Basset W

Mulcaster Avd

Dukes Rd

St Johns Dr

Brasenose Dr

PO

Evans La

Orchard Wy

Honor Close

Florence Cl

Green Way

White Way

Blenheim Road

Evans Ct

Beagles Cl

Cleveland

North Kidlington School

Kidlington Health Cen

Kidlington Parish Council

High St

Sterling Rd

Sterling Cl

Exeter Road

Old Chapel Street

School Road

St Marys Dr

The Town

Vicarage Rd

Webb's Way

Petre Place

Franklin Cl

Spindlers

Manor Farm Wy

Freeborn Close

Lambs Close

St Mary's Cl

Foxdown Close

Benmead

Ben Cl

Mead Wy

Home

Helwys Pl

Park Av

Marlborough Av

Wise Av

The Moors Road

Meadow Vw

Wolsey Rd

Yarnton Ct

Treeground Pl

Morton Cl

Churchill Road

Hardwick Avenue

Copthorne Rd

Cherry Cl

Rowanne Cl

Spruce Rd

Holly Cl

Ash

Maple

Almond Av

Furnium

Hazel

Beech Crs

Lock Cr

Strat

Elm Gv

Crescent Drive

Fairfax Rd

Hampden Drive

Astley Av

Cromwell Way

Gosford Close

St Thomas More RC School

West Kidlington Primary School

Gosford Hill School

Gosford Hill Medical Cen

Edward Field Primary School

Kidlington & Gosford Sports Centre

Greystones

Nurseries Rd

Crown Rd

Court Cl

The Phelps

Calves

Bellenger Wy

Broad Cl

Osborne

Grovelands

Newport Cl

Harts Cl

Claremont

Rutters

The Phelps

7

21

14

A · **B** Hampton Corse · **C** · D3 1 Conyer Cl · **D**

Field Barn Farm

B4027

BLETCHINGDON

1

Bletchingdon R

A34(T)

Oxford Road

2

3

13

The S

Kidlington Road

LC

Mill Farm

Mill

ermead

Queens Avenue

4

A34(T)

Bicester

Drive

ss Way

Beagles Cl

Water Cl

5

Eaton Lane

Northfield Farm

A · **B** · **22** · **C** · **D**

LC

E3
1 The Walk

E   F   G   H

I

Chipping
Farm

Brookfurlong
Farm

2

Oxfordshire Way

Islip
Station
Primary
School

Islip

Hilltop
Cres

North St

Middle
Way

HIGH
ST

Middle Street

1

Lower Street

KING'S HEAD LA

3

River Ray

Collice
Street

Bridge Street

WHEATLEY ROAD

4

Oxfordshire Way

B4027

5

Noke

23

E   F   G   H

Oxfordshire Way

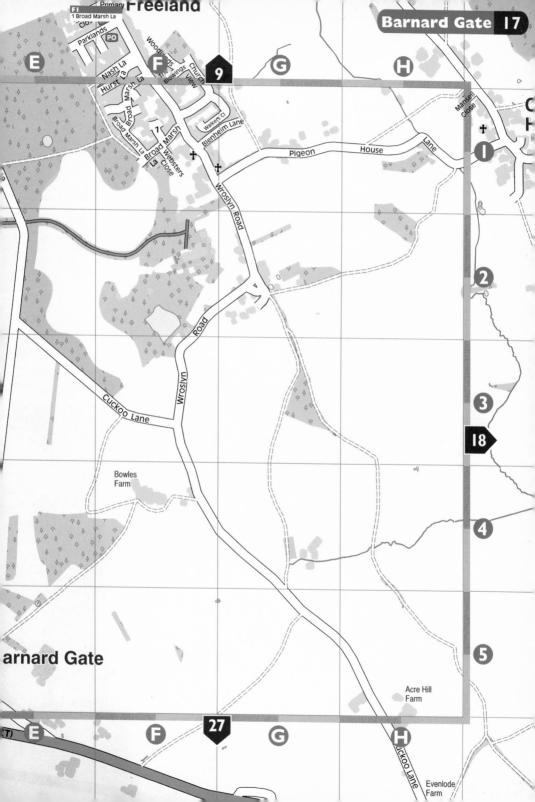

F1
1 Broad Marsh La

Primary

Clo

Parklands

PO

Nash La

Hurst La

Woodlands

The Blowings

Church View

E

F

G

9

H

Broad Marsh La

Broad Marsh La

17

Broad Marsh

Websters Close

Walkers Cl

Blenheim Lane

Pigeon   House   Lane

Mansell Close

I

Wroslyn Road

2

3

18

Wroslyn   Road

Cuckoo Lane

Bowles Farm

4

5

arnard Gate

Acre Hill Farm

(T)

E

F

27

G

H

Cuckoo Lane

Evenlode Farm

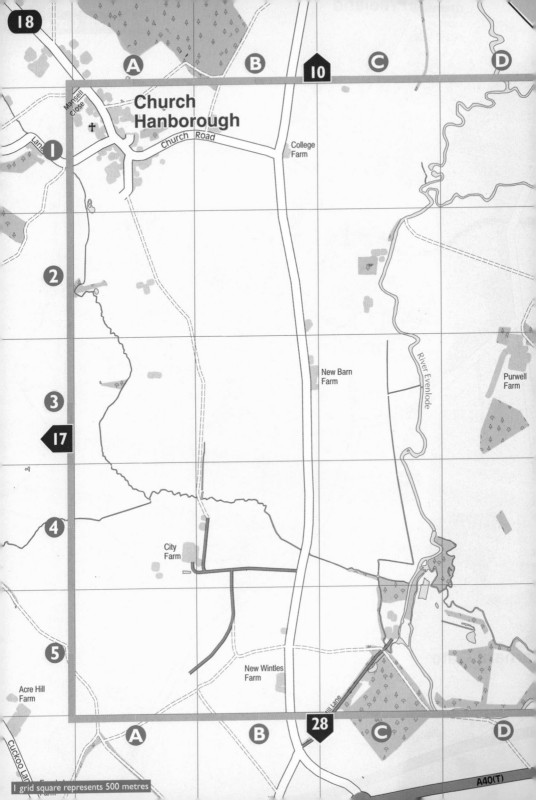

F5
1 Orchard Cl

E   F   H   G   H

Begbroke
Wood

Burleigh
Farm

Spring
Hill

I

2

3

20

Jericho
Barns

Worton

Yarnton Road

4

Yarnton Road

Elms
Road

The Green

Tennis

Bell

Bell Cl

Lynton
Lane

5

PO

St Peters
C of E
School

St Peter's

Cassington

Hollow
Furlong

Church Lane

Pound
Lane

Lane Horsemere
Lane

A40(T)

Eynsham Road

Manor Cl

borough
ve

A40(T)

E   F   29   G   H

A40(T)

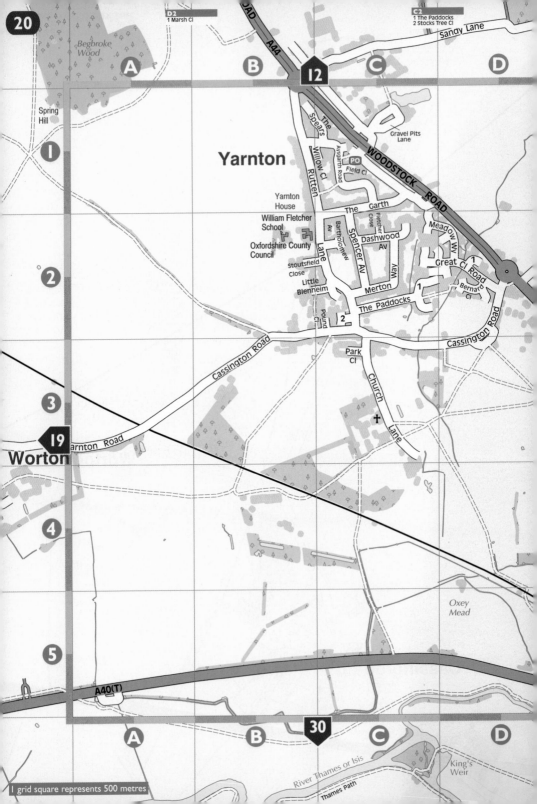

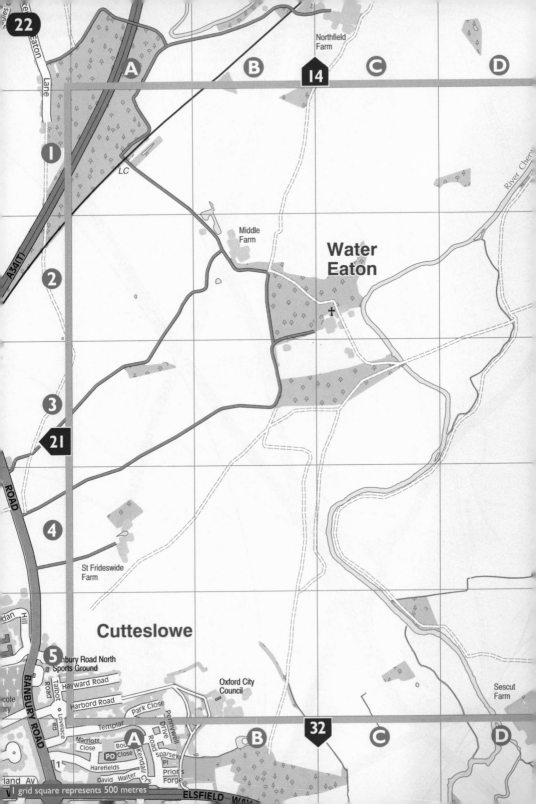

22

A

B

Northfield
Farm

C

14

D

1

Eaton Lane

LC

Middle
Farm

**Water
Eaton**

River Chen

2

A34 (T)

3

21

4

St Frideswide
Farm

ROAD

Cutteslowe

5

BANBURY ROAD

nbury Road North
Sports Ground

Oxford City
Council

Sescut
Farm

Talbot Road

Hayward Road

Harbord Road

Park Close

Lovelace Rd

Templar

Pennwell Drive

Marriott
Close

Bou
Close

Kendall Cs

sparsey
Pl

Priors
Forge

A

PO

1

Harefields

David Walter

B

32

C

D

ELSFIELD WAY

1 grid square represents 500 metres

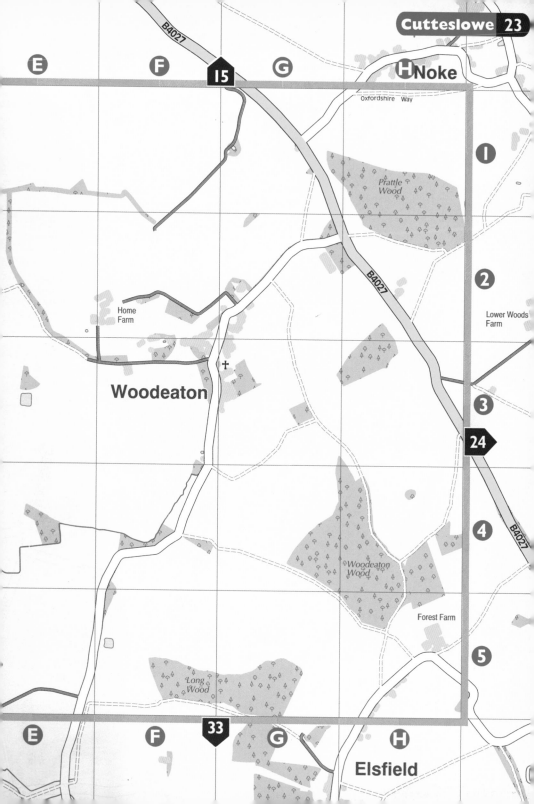

B4027

E　F　**15**　G　**H** Noke

Oxfordshire Way

I

Prattle
Wood

B4027

2

Lower Woods
Farm

Home
Farm

3

Woodeaton

24

4

B4027

Woodeaton
Wood

Forest Farm

5

Long
Wood

E　F　**33**　G　**H**

Elsfield

E F G H

I

2

3

The Spinney

Oxfordshire Way

4

Oxfordshire Way

Street

Middle
Park Farm

Beckley

*Blackwater
Wood*

*Stanton
Little
Wood*

Oxfordshire Way

5

Woodperry

Beckley
Court

Road

Bungalow Close

E F 35 Woodperry G H

*Holly
Wood*

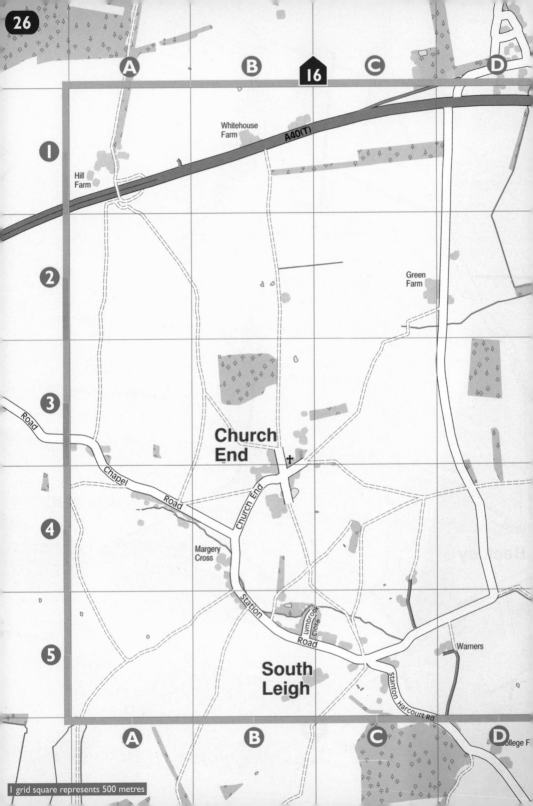

A   B   16   C   D

Whitehouse
Farm
A40(T)

1 Hill
Farm

2 Green
Farm

3 Road

Chapel

**Church
End**

Road

4 Margery
Cross   Church End

5 Station   Lymbrook
Cross   Warners

Road

**South
Leigh**   Stanton Harcourt Rd

A   B   C   D   ollege F

arnard Gate

E   F   **17**   G   H

I

Acre Hill Farm

Cuckoo Lane

Evenlode Farm

A40(T)

Old Witney Road

Tilgarsley Road

Fruitlands

EYNSHAM   **2**

Bartholomew Close

Willows Edge

Witney

Thornbury Road

Chil Brook

Twelve Acre Farm

Chilbridge   Road

3

28

4

Lower Farm

B4449

5

Foxley Farm

E   F   Limb Brook   G   H

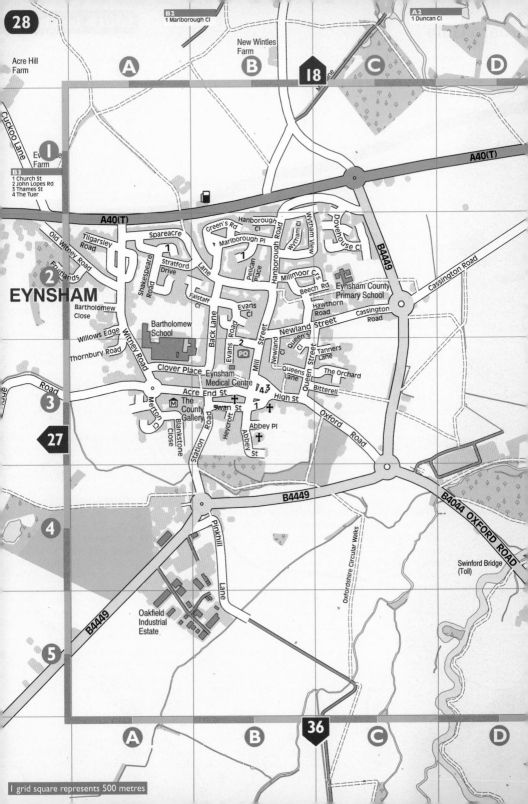

B2
1 Marlborough Cl

A2
1 Duncan Cl

A   B   18   C   D

Acre Hill
Farm

New Wintles
Farm

CUCKOO LANE

Evenlode
Farm

B3
1 Church St
2 John Lopes Rd
3 Thames St
4 The Tuer

A40(T)

A40(T)

Tilgarsley
Road

Old Witney Road

Spareacre

Green's Rd

Hanborough
Cl

Marlborough Pl

Wytham View

Dovehouse Cl

B4449

Cassington Road

Fruitlands

EYNSHAM

Bartholomew
Close

Shakespeare Road

Stratford
Drive

Falstaff
Cl

Back Lane

Pelican
Place

Hanborough Road

Wytham Road

Millmoor Crs

Beech Rd

Eynsham County
Primary School

Willows Edge

Thornbury Road

Witney Road

Bartholomew
School

Evans Road

Evans
Cl

Evans
Cl

Street

Newland

Newland Street

Queen's
Cl

Hawthorn
Road

Cassington
Road

Tanners
Lane

The Orchard

Clover Place

Eynsham
Medical Centre

Acre End St

Merton Cl

The
County
Gallery

Swan St

Blankstone
Close

Station Road

Heycroft

PO

Queens
Lane

Queen Street

Bitterell

High St

Oxford Road

27

3

Abbey Pl

Abbey
St

4

B4449

B4449

Pinkhill Lane

Oxfordshire Circular Walks

B4044 OXFORD ROAD

Swinford Bridge
(Toll)

Oakfield
Industrial
Estate

A   B   36   C   D

1 grid square represents 500 metres

Cassington

E

St Peters
PO C of E
School
St Peter's

Hollow
Fur
F
Church Lane

Eynsham Road

Manor Cl

Marlborough
Drive

19

A40(T)

7 Bell

Lane Horse Fair

Lane

G

H

A40(T)

I

2

River Thames or Isis

3

30

Wytham
Great
Wood

4

Swinford

5

The Five
Sisters

E

F

37

G

H

Radbrook
Common

30

A40(T) **A**

B

20

C

D

River Thames or Isis

King's Weir

Thames Path

Thames Path

I

Thames Path

2

3

29

A34(T)

4

Wytham

PO

PH

5

Wytham Park

A34(T)

A

B

38

C

D

A34(T)

Marley Wood

1 grid square represents 500 metres

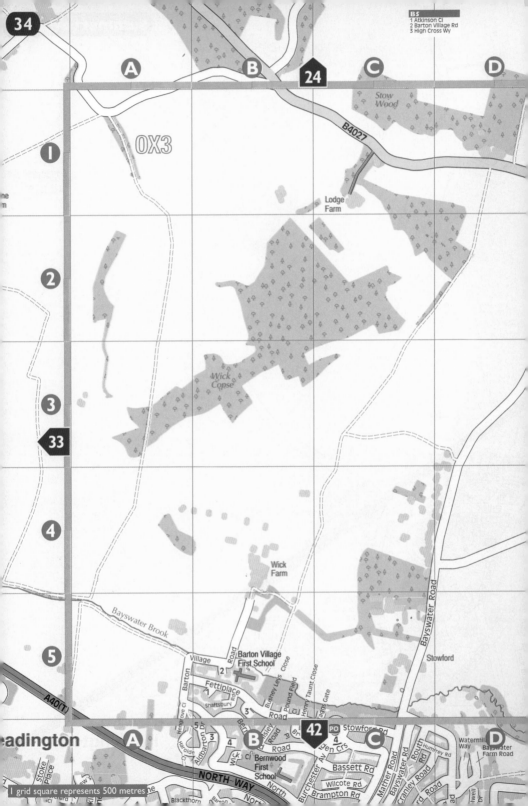

E F **25** G H

Woodperry

I

New Inn
Farm

B4027

2

Pound Lane

Mill Street

Middle Road

Cocks Lane

PO

**Stanton
St John**

Hillcraft Rd

3

PH

PH

Courtfield
Road

Shepherds
Pit

4

B4027

Ashen
Copse

5

E F **43** G H Ixie Way STANTON ROAD Polecat End WHR

Bungalow Close

Road

Holly
Wood

Milton CFS

Powell Close

Manor
Farm

Sandhills

36

A **B** **28** **C** **D**

I

2

Pinkhill Farm

Lower
Whitley
Farm

Thames   Path

3

4

5

A **B** **46** **C** **D**

Thames or Isis

hames Path

I grid square represents 500 metres

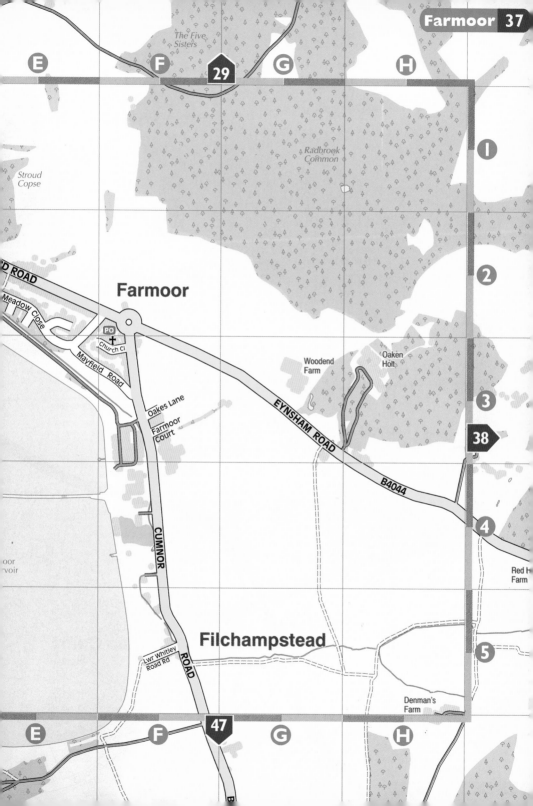

The Five Sisters

E   F   **29**   G   H

I

Stroud
Copse

Radbrook
Common

2

Farmoor

PO
Church Cl

Meadow Close

Mayfield Road

Woodend
Farm

Oaken
Holt

3

Oakes Lane

Farmoor
Court

EYNSHAM ROAD

38

B4044

4

CUMNOR

Red H
Farm

oor
voir

ROAD

Filchampstead

5

Lwr Whitley
Road Rd

Denman's
Farm

E   F   **47**   G   H

38

30

C4
W 1 Deanfield Rd
Park

B5
1 Browns Cl
2 Stubble Cl

A34(T)

A   **B**   **C**   **D**

I

D5
1 Springfield Rd

Marley Wood

OX2

2

3

Tilbury Farm

37

Tilbury Lane

A420(T)

4

Botley

Bot
Me
Cer

Red House Farm

Fogwell Rd
Honestall
Portle Cl
Stone Cl
Road
Bushey Cl
Long Cl
Broad Cl
Owlington Cl

Hazel Rd

Seacourt Road

Tudor Court

Nobles Lane

A420(T)

Orchard Road

Sumpsons Cl
Fogwell
Ashcroft Cl
Grange

1

Rose Gdns

Conifer Cl

Wes
Hea
Cer

EYNSHAM ROAD

B4044

Evelyn Close

Dean Court

5

Nobles Cl
Green La
Pinnocks Wy

Third Acre Rise

Pinnocks

Queens Cl

Cumnor Hill

Hurst Rise Road

Cumnor Rise Road

Denton Close

Denman's Farm

2
1

Pinnocks Way

Dean Rd

Stanville Rd

1

A   **B**   **C**   **D**

48

Arnold's
cholan
Way

High

1 grid square represents 500 metres

E4
1 Chapel Wy
2 Elms Pde

E5
1 The Garth
2 Hawthorne Cl
3 Maple Cl
4 St Paul's Crs

Binsey

Thames or Isis

Thames Path

Aristotle Lane

Plater Drive

Rutherway

Walton Well Rd

PO
PH

First School
St Margaret's Rd

Walt Manor

G4
1 Marlborough Ct

I

Tackley Pl

Leckford

Plantation

St Bern

Wellbei Clinic

2

Jericho H1
1 Merrivale Sq

First School

Cranham

Jericho

Clarendon St

Nelson Street

3

Seacourt Stream

Binsey Lane

River Thames or Isis

Thames Path

A420

P+

Prestwich Pl

West Oxford Health Centre

Bulstake Cl

Helen Rd

Henry Rd

Oxfo Stn

40

H3
1 Combe Rd
2 Dawson Pl
3 Mount Pl

Business School

4

Lamarsh Road

Earl St

Duke St

Riverside Rd

Harley Rd

Oatlands Rd

Alexandra Rd

PO

Hillview Rd

Hinksey

Ferry Rd

A420 BOTLEY ROAD

University of Oxford

Mill Street

Arthur St

Bridge St

West St

East St

Osney

Abbey Rd

Cripley Road

P

H4
1 Cripley Pl
2 Russell St

HYTH

New Botley

Primary School

Swan St

South St

Doyley Rd

Electric Avenue

Barrett Street

Millbank

Holywell Business Centre

Osney

Osney Lane

College

Cem

Oxford Business Centre

Hinksey Business Centre

Cemetery

SOUTHERN

Yarnell's Road

North Hinksey Lane

WESTMINSTER

Crozier Cl

BY-PASS Way

North Hinksey C of E School

Raleigh Park Rd

Osney Mead Industrial Estate

Osney Mead

Thames Path

5

A34(T) ROAD

North Hinksey

E   F   G   H

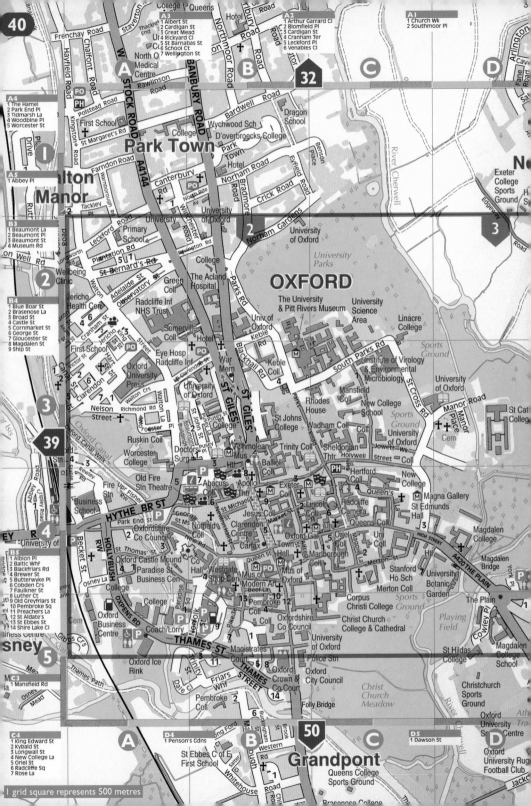

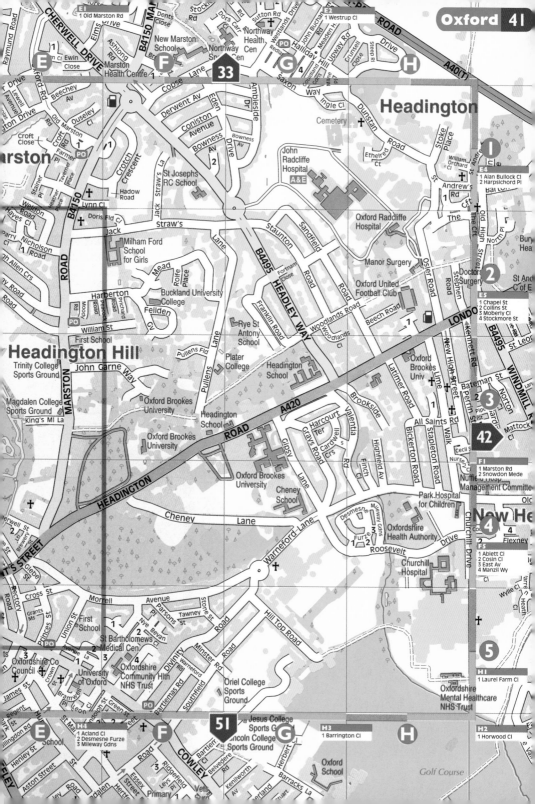

E **F** **35** **G** **H**

I

Mickle Way

STANTON ROAD

Polecat En

Milton

W R

Sandhills

Sandhills
County Primary
School

Manor
Farm

Cemetery

✝

2

A40(T)

OAD

LONDON ROAD

Thornhill Farm

rst

3

44

4

Shotover Plain

Old Road

Littleworth

5

Acremead Rd

Acremead Road

Keydale Rd

Kelly's

Westhill
Farm

Horspath
Common

E **F** **53** **G** **H**

Blenheim Road

Blenheim

nheim Wy

Filchampstead

H4
1 Abingdon Rd
2 Kenilworth Rd
3 Robsart Pl

E F **37** G H

Denman's Farm

I

2

Lwr Whitley Road Rd

ROAD

B4017

A4

TUMBLEDOWN HILL

Upper Whitley Farm

Leys Road

Long Leys Farm

Denman's Lane

Cumnor C of E Primary School

Norrey

Bertle Road

PO

3

ford

HIGH STREET

PH

Cumnor

PH

GLEBE RD

The Glebe

A42

48

Cumnor

The Winnyards

Road

The Park

2 Forster Lane

1

4

Appleton

Robsart Place

Robsart Place

ton

tice

FARINGDON ROAD

Bradley Farm

5

B4017

E F **57** G H

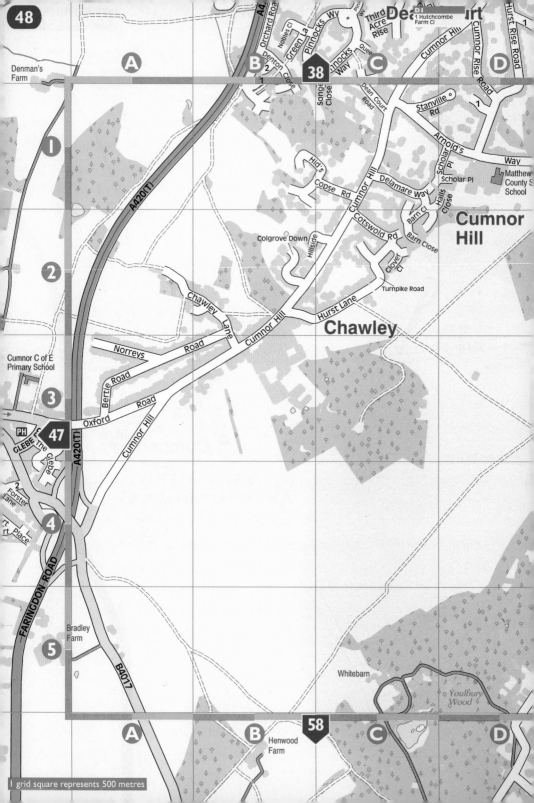

E **F** **G** **H**

1 Westminster Wy

Westminster

BY-PASS

Crozier Cl

Sweetmans Rd

Yarnell's

Brogden Cl

Raleigh Park Rd

Way

North Hinksey Village

Harcourt Hill

College

Harcourt

Stanton Rd

Vernon Avenue

Grosvenor Road

Harcourt Hill

Crabtree Rd

Laburnum Rd

more Rd

h Road

Lime Road

tnut

Hinksey Lane

39

A34(T) ROAD

Oxford Rugby
Football Club

Osney Mead
Industrial
Estat

Osney
Mead

Thames Path

I

Hinksey Stream

2

A34(T)

SOUTHERN

Hinksey Hill
Farm

3

PASS

50

4

OX1

Chilswell
Farm

Chilswell
House (Priory)

5

Chilswell

Lane

E **F** 59 **G** **H**

Chilswell Lane Road

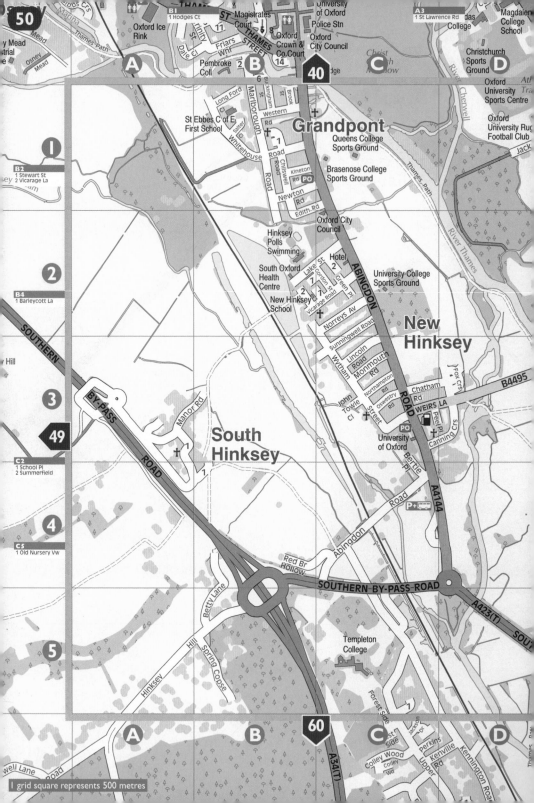

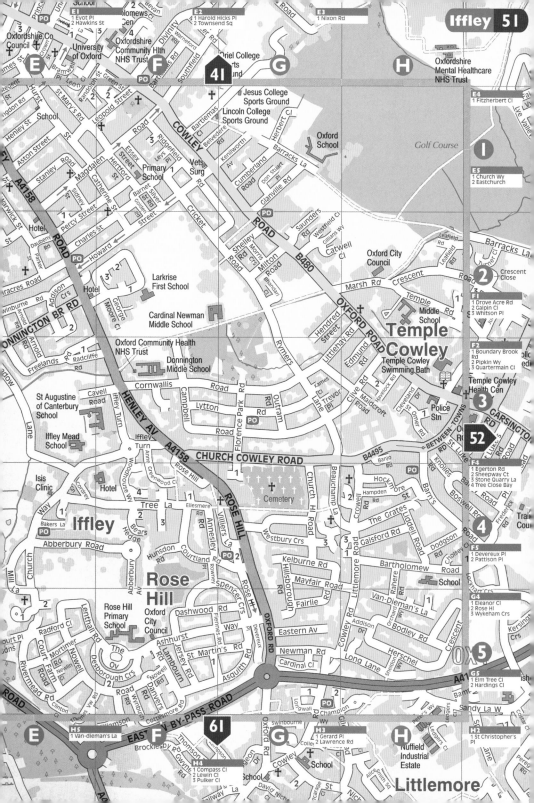

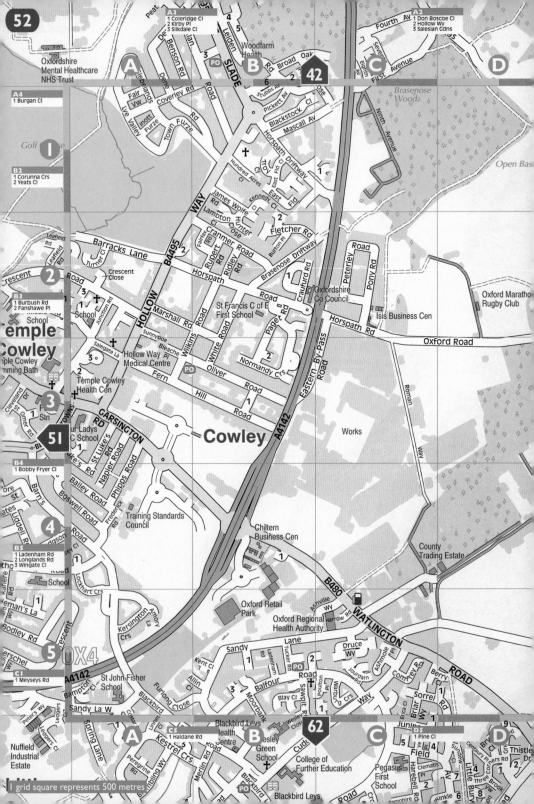

Holton Mill

E F **45** G H

M40

Wheatley Bridge

A40(T)

I

Jun

Oxford Service Area

2

Sworford Lane

River Thame

M40

3

Cuddesdon Brook

4

Sworford Lane

5

Lower

Pott's

E F **65** G H

Cuddesdon

A   B   46   C   D

I

2

3

River Thames or Isis

Thames Path

Thames Path

Appleton

Badswell
Lane
Town
Southby
Whites
Furlong Forge
Church
Rd
PO
Park
Ma
Ho

Thames Path

4

5

Appleton
Lower
Common

Millway   Lane

Netherton Road

Field
Farm

A   B   C   D

E   F   **47**   G   H

B4017

I

2   Hen

Eaton Road

Bessels Leigh

A420(T)

3

Bessels Leigh Road

58

4

Tubney
Manor Farm

Bessels Leigh
School

†

Great Park
Farm

5

Row Leigh Lane

Dry Sand
Primary S

E   F   pwood
Park   G   H   †

The Ride

A420(T)   A338   The Ride

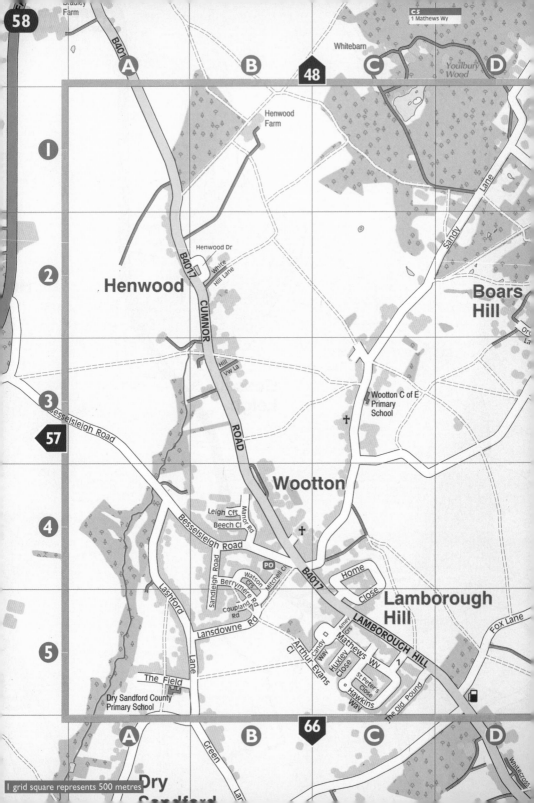

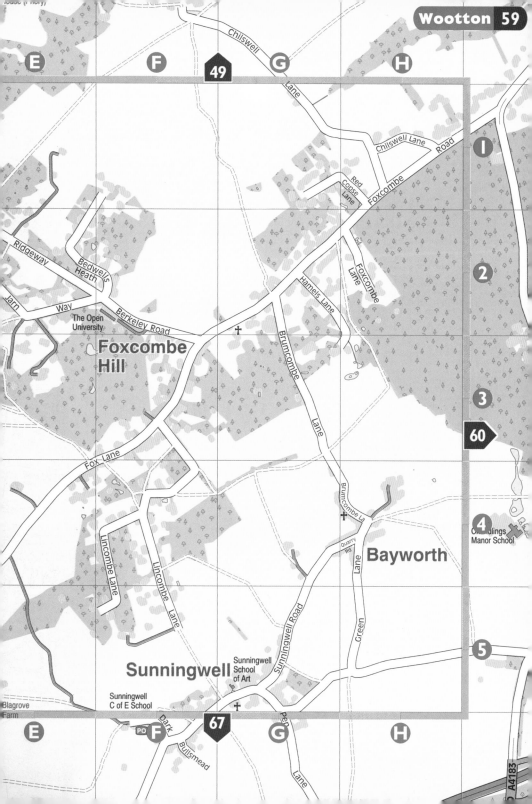

E F G H

49

Chiswell Lane

I

Chilswell Lane

Red Copse Lane

Foxcombe Road

2

Ridgeway

Bedwells Heath

Jarn

Way

Berkeley Road

The Open University

Hamels Lane

Foxcombe Lane

Foxcombe Hill

Brumcombe

3

60

Fox Lane

Lane

Brumcombe La

Lincombe Lane

Lincombe Lane

Quarry Rd

Bayworth

4

Chaundings Manor School

5

Sunningwell

Sunningwell School of Art

Sunningwell Road

Green

Lane

Blagrove Farm

Sunningwell C of E School

PO F

Dark

67

G

Pen

H

Bullsmead

Lane

A4183

E

60

D4
1 Bluebell Ride
2 Hazelnut Pth

Templeton
College

D1
1 Blackman Cl

SOU

Hinksey

A **B** **50** **C** **D**

well Lane

1

Forest
Side

Jackson

Colley Wood

Perkins

Kenville
Rd

Kennington Road

D5
1 Sugworth Crs

de

Colley
Wd

Upper

Road

7

PO

Bagley Close

Bagley
Close

Edward
Road

Rowles

Kennington
Health Cen

2 *Bagley Wood*

**Little
London**

Woodcroft

Bagley Wood Rd

Doctors
Surgery

Cow

K

St Swithuns
C of E
Primary
School

Grundy
Crs

The

River
VW

3

Oxford Road

KIRK
Cl

St
Swithun's
Road

Avenue

59

Simpsons Wy

The Av

Links Rd

Liddla
d Cl

4

Chandlings
Manor School

Bagley Wood Road

Playfield Road

Cranbrook Dr

The
Paddock

Willow
Way

Sycamore Crs

1

2

Oak
Blossoms
Gld

Av

Sugworth
Farm

5

Sugworth Lane

Sugworth Lane

A **B** **68** **C** **D**

A34(T)

183

1 grid square represents 500 metres

H2
1 Sadlers Cft

Oxford Road

E   F   53   G   H

I

Poplar
Cl
Poplar Cft

PO   Birch
Road

Blenheim

Elm

Willow
Cl

Larch End

Kiln Farm

Combewell

Lane

Fox
Close

Wheatley Road

Garsington C of E
Primary School

Garsington
Sports Club

Denton Lane

WATLINGTON

Kiln

The
HI

1

The Hill

Alpha   Avenue

The Gn

Garsingto 2

ROAD

Southend

B480

Pettiwell

3 **South**

64

4

Southend

B480

5

PH

Lower
Farm

**Toot
Baldon**

E

D2
1 Partridge Wk
2 Rowan Gv

F   71   G   H

don

V

64

Ⓐ

Ⓑ

54

Ⓒ
Church
Close

Cuddesdo

Ⓓ

The Gr

Ⓘ

Upperfield
Farm

High St.
PH
The Lane

Denton Hill

Wheatley Road

Garsington
Sports Club

Denton Lane

Denton Lane

Denton

Garsi2gton

Denton Lane

3

Southend

63

The Platt

4

Southend

5

B480

Lower
Farm

Hill
Farm

Ⓐ

Ⓑ

Ⓒ

Ⓓ

I grid square represents 500 metres

G4
1 Chiltern Vw
2 Warren Vw

55

E F G H

I

Cuddesdon
Mill

The
Forties

The
Views

2

River Thame

Lower

Pott's Cl

Chu...

The
Sands

A329

3

4

THAME ROAD

2

Old
Fld

A329

1

PO

Belcher's
Farm

Church Hill

Haseley Rd

5

Gold St

Blenheim Rd

Little Milton
School

Little Milton

E F G H

Ditchend
Farm

68

A   B   **60**   C   D

A34(T)

Oxford A4183 Road

Sugworth Lane

I

2

3

67

4

5

Radley Park

The Infirmary

Radley College

Chestnut Av

Kennington Road

Radle Prima

Radley

Twelve Acre Drive

Twelve Acre Drive

White's

Ferry Close

St James

Foxborough

Gooseacre

Badgers Copse

Peachcroft Shopping Centre

College Oak

Peachcroft

Norfolk Close

Drysdale Close

Radley Road

Goose Acre Farm

Rush Common County Primary School

Radley Rd

The Copse

Radley

The Chestnuts

Audlett Drive

Thrupp Road

Norman Avenue

Doctors Surgery

Special School

Primary School

74

Home Farm

Lane

1 grid square represents 500 metres

E3
1 Catherine Cl

Lower
Farm

A4074

E

F

61

G

H

I

Thames Path

2

Thames Path

3

Upper F

70

4

Lower Radley

's Copse

Radley Station

N

5

Thames Path

Nuneham
House

E

F

75

G

H

Pumney
Farm

PH

E Toot
Baldon

F

63

G

H wer
Farm

I

Gotham Farm

2

3

Marylands Farm

4

B4015

Marylands Gn

e Baldon Farm

5

Baldon Brook

E

F

77

G

H

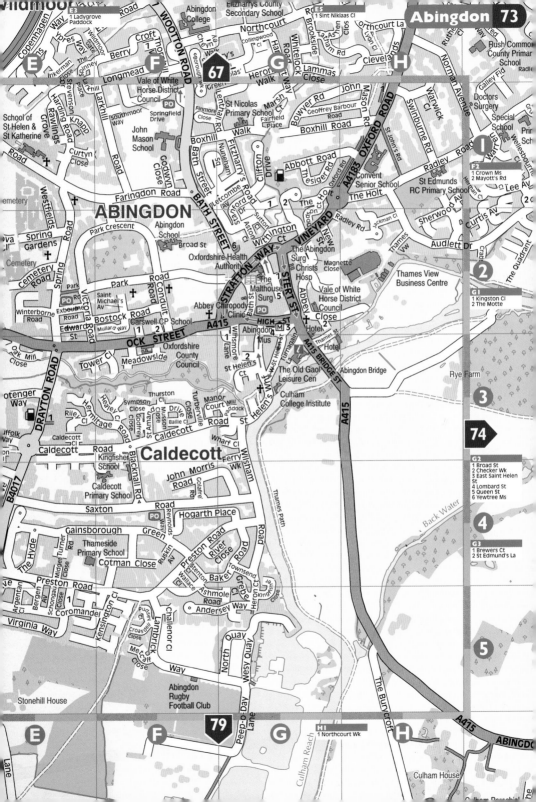

Nuneham House

E   F   **69**   G   H

Pumney Farm

I

Roundh Wood

Lock Wood

2

Thames Path

The Coppice

3

76

Furze Brake

4

Thame Lane

Lane

Courtiers Green

The Culham Laboratory

Clifton Hampden

5

Watery Lane

Th

PH

Clifton Hampden C.of E. Primary School

PO

Station

Station Road

High Street

76

A   B   **70**   C   D

1

Roundhill
Wood

*Clifton
Heath*

Golden Balls

A4074

2

B4015

The Coppice

OXFORD   ROAD

3

Burcot
Farm

75

4

A415   ABINGDON   ROAD

Burcot Park   **Burcot**

P

Courtiers
Green

**Clifton
Hampden**

Watery
Lane

The Surgery

River Thames or Isis

Thai

PH

Clifton
Hampden C. of E
Primary School

PO

Thames Path

High Street

A   B   C   D

Northfield Farm

F3
1 Pritchard Cl

E   F   71   G   Baldon Brook   H

I

2

3

Barrington Cl
Russell Jackson Cl
Crutch Furlong
Fane Dr
Tower Rd
1
Evenlode Dr
Cherwell Road
Glyme Drive
Fane Drive
West Cft
Fane Drive
Lav Av
Colne Drive
Berinsfield Health Centre
PO
Colwell Rd
Ock Dr
Green Furlong
Berinsfield
Leach Rd
Shadwell Road
Abbey Sports Centre
Abbey Woods Cl
Wey Rd
Mount Farm
Bullingdon Avenue
Wimblestraw Rd
Chiltern Cl
Primary School
Loddon Av
Fane Drive
Windrush Rd
Kennet Close
A4074

4

5

Burcot Lane

E   F   G   H

Abingdon Road
Dorchester Sailing Club
Road

72

A B C D

1

2

3

4

5

A B C D

Drayton

Sutton

ABINGDON ROAD

Corneville Road

Lyford Cl.

C.B.S.E.

Primary School

Crabtree Lane

Greenacres

Newman Lane

Meads Cl.

Rippington Cl.

Sutton Wick Lane

Gilbourn's Farm

Henleys Lane

Fisher Close

Hilliat Fields

Manor Cl.

Caudwell Close

Church Lane

Marcham Road

PO

B4017

Gravel Lane

HIGH STREET

B4016

Halls Close

Chiers Close

Chiers Farm

Whitehorns Way

Steventon Road

LOCKWAY

A34(T)

Doctors Surgery

East Way

STEVENTON ROAD

Haywards Road

Drayton Golf Club

B4017

A   B   74   C OX14   D

A415

ABINGDON   ROAD

Culham House

1

Culham Parochial
Primary School

The Glebe

Tollgate Road

The Burycroft

Culham

2

ulham Cut

Abingdon Road

Sutton
Pools

Thames

PH

APPLEFORD ROAD B4016

Saints Lane

3

CHURCH STREET

79

All

Churchmere
Road

Church Ml
Rd

Sutton Courtenay

4

Bridg

Applefor

5

Hobbyhorse   Lane

A   B   C   D

1 grid square represents 500 metres

The Culham Laboratory

Clifton Hampden C of E Primary School

Culham Station

Station Road

Zouch Farm

Fullamoor

High Street

Long Wittenham C of E Primary School

Long Wittenham

Clifton Lock

Thames Path

Clifton Cut

School Lane

Church St

Appleford

High Str

Fieldside

Didcot Road

Westfield Road

PO

Pendon Museum

E F 75 G H

I

2

3

4

5

E F G H

Abingdon	73 F2	Cumnor	47 G3	Kennington	60 D2	Sandhills	
Abingdon Bridge	73 F3	Cumnor Hill	48 D2	Kidlington	13 F3	Shippon	
Appleford	81 E4	Cutteslowe	22 A5	Lamborough Hill	58 C5	Shipton-on-Cherwell	
Appleton	56 C4	Dean Court	38 C5	Little London	60 C2	Southend	
Baldon Row	70 D1	Denton	64 C2	Little Milton	65 H5	South Hinksey	
Barnard Gate	17 E5	Drayton	78 C4	Littlemore	61 H1	South Leigh	
Barton	42 C1	Dry Sandford	66 A1	Littleworth	43 H5	Stanton St John	
Bayworth	59 H4	East End	8 C2	Long Hanborough	9 H3	Summertown	
Beckley	25 E4	East End	10 A1	Long Wittenham	81 H4	Sunningwell	
Begbroke	12 A3	Eaton	47 E5	Lower Radley	69 F4	Sunnymead	
Berinsfield	77 F4	Elsfield	33 H1	Marsh Baldon	70 C3	Sutton Courtenay	
Bessels Leigh	57 G3	Eynsham	27 H2	Marston	32 D4	Sutton Wick	
Binsey	39 F1	Farmoor	37 F2	New Botley	39 F4	Swinford	
Blackbird Leys	62 A2	Filchampstead	37 F5	New Headington	42 A4	Temple Cowley	
Bladon	11 F2	Forest Hill	44 A1	New Hinksey	50 C2	Thrupp	
Blenheim	53 F1	Foxcombe Hill	59 F3	New Marston	40 D1	Toot Baldon	
Blenheim	63 G1	Freeland	9 F5	Noke	15 H5	Upper Wolvercote	
Boars Hill	58 D2	Garsington	63 H2	Northcourt	67 H4	Walton Manor	
Botley	38 D4	Golden Balls	76 B1	North Hinksey Village	49 F1	Water Eaton	
Bunkers Hill	6 C1	Gosford	13 G5	North Leigh	8 A5	Waterperry	
Burcot	76 C5	Grandpont	50 B1	Nuneham Courtenay	70 B3	West End	
Caldecott	73 F3	Hampton Gay	7 E4	Old Woodstock	4 D1	Wheatley	
Campsfield	11 H2	Hampton Poyle	13 H1	Osney	39 H5	Wildmoor	
Cassington	19 E5	Harcourt Hill	49 F2	Oxford	3 G5	Wolvercote	
Chawley	48 C2	Headington	41 H1	Park Town	40 A1	Woodeaton	
Church End	26 B3	Hensington	5 F2	The Platt	64 B4	Woodstock	
Church Hanborough	18 A1	Henwood	58 A2	Radley	68 D4	Wootton	
Clifton Hampden	75 H5	Holton	44 D4	Radley Park	68 B2	Worton	
Cowley	52 B3	Horspath	53 G2	Risinghurst	42 D2	Wytham	
Cuddesdon	54 D5	Iffley	51 E4	Rose Hill	51 F4	Yarnton	
Culham	79 H2	Islip	15 E3	Sandford-on-Thames	61 G4		

USING THE STREET INDEX

Street names are listed alphabetically. Each street name is followed by its postal town or area locality, the Postcode District, the page number, and the reference to the square in which the name is found.

Example: **Abbots Wood (East)** *HEAD* OX3.................... **42** B5 **1**

Some entries are followed by a number in a blue box. This number indicates the location of the street within the referenced grid square. The full street name is listed at the side of the map page.

GENERAL ABBREVIATIONS

ACC	ACCESS	DL	DALE	IN	INLET	PL	
ALY	ALLEY	DM	DAM	IND EST	INDUSTRIAL ESTATE	PLN	
AP	APPROACH	DR	DRIVE	INF	INFIRMARY	PLNS	
AR	ARCADE	DRO	DROVE	INFO	INFORMATION	PLZ	
ASS	ASSOCIATION	DRY	DRIVEWAY	INT	INTERCHANGE	POL	POLICE
AV	AVENUE	DWGS	DWELLINGS	IS	ISLAND	PR	
BCH	BEACH	E	EAST	JCT	JUNCTION	PREC	P
BLDS	BUILDINGS	EMB	EMBANKMENT	JTY	JETTY	PREP	PREPA
BND	BEND	EMBY	EMBASSY	KG	KING	PRIM	F
BNK	BANK	ESP	ESPLANADE	KNL	KNOLL	PROM	PRO
BR	BRIDGE	EST	ESTATE	L	LAKE	PRS	P
BRK	BROOK	EX	EXCHANGE	LA	LANE	PRT	
BTM	BOTTOM	EXPY	EXPRESSWAY	LDG	LODGE	PT	
BUS	BUSINESS	EXT	EXTENSION	LGT	LIGHT	PTH	
BVD	BOULEVARD	F/O	FLYOVER	LK	LOCK	PZ	
BY	BYPASS	FC	FOOTBALL CLUB	LKS	LAKES	QD	QU
CATH	CATHEDRAL	FK	FORK	LNDG	LANDING	QU	
CEM	CEMETERY	FLD	FIELD	LTL	LITTLE	QY	
CEN	CENTRE	FLDS	FIELDS	LWR	LOWER	R	
CFT	CROFT	FLS	FALLS	MAG	MAGISTRATE	RBT	ROUN
CH	CHURCH	FLS	FLATS	MAN	MANSIONS	RD	
CHA	CHASE	FM	FARM	MD	MEAD	RDG	
CHYD	CHURCHYARD	FT	FORT	MDW	MEADOWS	REP	R
CIR	CIRCLE	FWY	FREEWAY	MEM	MEMORIAL	RES	RE
CIRC	CIRCUS	FY	FERRY	MKT	MARKET	RFC	RUGBY FOOTBA
CL	CLOSE	GA	GATE	MKTS	MARKETS	RI	
CLFS	CLIFFS	GAL	GALLERY	ML	MALL	RP	
CMP	CAMP	GDN	GARDEN	ML	MILL	RW	
CNR	CORNER	GDNS	GARDENS	MNR	MANOR	S	
CO	COUNTY	GLD	GLADE	MS	MEWS	SCH	
COLL	COLLEGE	GLN	GLEN	MSN	MISSION	SE	SOU
COM	COMMON	GN	GREEN	MT	MOUNT	SER	SERVI
COMM	COMMISSION	GND	GROUND	MTN	MOUNTAIN	SH	
CON	CONVENT	GRA	GRANGE	MTS	MOUNTAINS	SHOP	SH
COT	COTTAGE	GRG	GARAGE	MUS	MUSEUM	SKWY	
COTS	COTTAGES	GT	GREAT	MWY	MOTORWAY	SMT	
CP	CAPE	GTWY	GATEWAY	N	NORTH	SOC	
CPS	COPSE	GV	GROVE	NE	NORTH EAST	SP	
CR	CREEK	HGR	HIGHER	NW	NORTH WEST	SPR	
CREM	CREMATORIUM	HL	HILL	O/P	OVERPASS	SQ	
CRS	CRESCENT	HLS	HILLS	OFF	OFFICE	ST	
CSWY	CAUSEWAY	HO	HOUSE	ORCH	ORCHARD	STN	
CT	COURT	HOL	HOLLOW	OV	OVAL	STR	
CTRL	CENTRAL	HOSP	HOSPITAL	PAL	PALACE	STRD	
CTS	COURTS	HRB	HARBOUR	PAS	PASSAGE	SW	SOU
CTYD	COURTYARD	HTH	HEATH	PAV	PAVILION	TDG	
CUTT	CUTTINGS	HTS	HEIGHTS	PDE	PARADE	TER	
CV	COVE	HVN	HAVEN	PH	PUBLIC HOUSE	THWY	THRO
CYN	CANYON	HWY	HIGHWAY	PK	PARK	TNL	
DEPT	DEPARTMENT	IMP	IMPERIAL	PKWY	PARKWAY	TOLL	

...TURNPIKE	UPR ...UPPER	VLG ...VILLAGE	WK ...WALK
...TRACK	V ...VALE	VLS ...VILLAS	WKS ...WALKS
...TRAIL	VA ...VALLEY	VW ...VIEW	WLS ...WELLS
...TOWER	VIAD ...VIADUCT	W ...WEST	WY ...WAY
...UNDERPASS	VIL ...VILLA	WD ...WOOD	YD ...YARD
...UNIVERSITY	VIS ...VISTA	WHF ...WHARF	YHA ...YOUTH HOSTEL

STCODE TOWNS AND AREA ABBREVIATIONS

...Abingdon	MCHM/KBPZ ...Marcham/Kingston Bagpuize	OXN/BOT/CM ...Oxford north/Botley/Cumnor	WGFD ...Wallingford
MR ...Cowley/Littlemore	OX/KTN ...Oxford/Kennington	STAD ...Stadhampton	WHLY ...Wheatley
...Headington		WDSTK ...Woodstock	WIT/EY ...Witney/Eynsham
...Kidlington			

dex - streets

A

Abb - Bra

A

ury Av COW/LTMR OX4 ...... 51 F5
ury Rd COW/LTMR OX4 ...... 51 E4
Cl ABGD OX14 ...... 73 G2
Pl OX/KTN OX1 ...... 2 B7
y OX8 ...... 28 B3
Rd OXN/BOT/CM OX2 ...... 39 H4
St WIT/EY OX8 ...... 28 B3
Woods Cl WGFD OX10 ...... 77 F4
Wood (East) HEAD OX3 .. 42 B5
Wood (West)
OX3 ...... 42 B5
Rd ABGD OX14 ...... 73 G1
od Rd WIT/EY OX8 ...... 9 F5
on Br ABGD OX14 ...... 73 G3
on Rd ABGD OX14 ...... 78 C2
OX14 ...... 80 A2
n OX1 ...... 50 C4
BOT/CM OX2 ...... 47 H4
OX10 ...... 77 E5
Cl COW/LTMR OX4 ...... 51 F1
Cl HEAD OX3 ...... 41 H4
ter Cl ABGD OX14 ...... 28 A3
dra Rd OXN/BOT/CM OX2 ...... 39 G4
st OX/KTN OX1 ...... 2 D6
mith Sq COW/LTMR OX4 ...... 61 H1
st OXN/BOT/CM OX2 ...... 2 A2
BOT/CM OX2 ...... 39 H2
l ABGD OX14 ...... 67 G4
ey Wy ABGD OX14 ...... 73 F5
ons Cl KID OX5 ...... 12 D4
neda Cl COW/LTMR OX4 .. 62 C2
e Cl COW/LTMR OX4 ...... 62 B3
COW/LTMR OX4 ...... 62 C2
avlova Cl ABGD OX14 ...... 73 E2
reenwood Cl
LTRMR OX4 ...... 51 F5
ey Cl KID OX5 ...... 7 H1
ey Rd COW/LTMR OX4 ...... 51 F4
y WHLY OX33 ...... 44 D5
ord Dr ABGD OX14 ...... 68 A4
ord Rd ABGD OX14 ...... 80 A3
on Rd OXN/BOT/CM OX2 ...... 47 G4
ree Cl COW/LTMR OX4 .. 62 C3
Rd OXN/BOT/CM OX2 ...... 31 H2
an Cl ABGD OX14 ...... 75 E1
COW/LTMR OX4 ...... 51 E1
le La OXN/BOT/CM OX2 ...... 39 H1
on Dr HEAD OX3 ...... 32 D5
s OX14 ...... 51 E3
s Wy OXN/BOT/CM OX2 ...... 48 C1
y Rd OXN/BOT/CM OX2 ...... 38 D5

Arthur Evans Cl
MCHM/KBPZ OX13 ...... 58 B5
Arthur Garrard Cl
OXN/BOT/CM OX2 ...... 2 B1
Arthur St OXN/BOT/CM OX2 ...... 39 H4
Ash Cl KID OX5 ...... 13 F5
Ashcroft Cl OXN/BOT/CM OX2 ...... 38 C4
Ashenden Cl ABGD OX14 ...... 67 G5
Ashford OX8 ...... 28 B3
Ash Gv HEAD OX3 ...... 42 A1
Ashhurst Wy COW/LTMR OX4 ...... 51 F5
Ashlong Rd HEAD OX3 ...... 33 F5
Ashmole Pl COW/LTMR OX4 ...... 52 C5
Ashmole Rd ABGD OX14 ...... 73 F5
Ashville Wy COW/LTMR OX4 ...... 52 B5
Aspen Sq COW/LTMR OX4 .. 62 B2
Astley Av KID OX5 ...... 21 G1
Aston Cl ABGD OX14 ...... 73 G2
Aston St OXN/BOT/CM OX2 ...... 51 E1
Atkinson Cl HEAD OX3 ...... 34 B5
Atkyns Rd HEAD OX3 ...... 42 B5
Atwell Pl HEAD OX3 ...... 42 A4
Audlett Dr ABGD OX14 ...... 73 H2
Austin Pl ABGD OX14 ...... 67 F4
Avenue La COW/LTMR OX4 ...... 60 D4
The Avenue OX/KTN OX1 ...... 3 K7
WHLY OX33 ...... 54 D1
Avon Rd MCHM/KBPZ OX13 ...... 66 B3
Axtell Cl KID OX5 ...... 13 E5
Aysgarth Rd KID OX5 ...... 20 C1
Azalea Av KID OX5 ...... 21 F1

B

Bablock Hythe Rd WIT/EY OX8 ...... 46 C3
Back La WIT/EY OX8 ...... 28 B3
Badgers Copse ABGD OX14 ...... 68 D4
Badswell La MCHM/KBPZ OX13 ...... 56 D3
Bagley Cl OXN/BOT/CM OX2 ...... 60 C2
Bagley Wood Rd OX/KTN OX1 ...... 60 B4
Bailey Rd COW/LTMR OX4 ...... 51 H4
Bailie Cl ABGD OX14 ...... 73 F3
Bainton Rd OXN/BOT/CM OX2 ...... 31 H5
Baker Cl HEAD OX3 ...... 42 C3
Baker Rd ABGD OX14 ...... 73 F4
Bakers La COW/LTMR OX4 ...... 51 E4
Baldon La STAD OX44 ...... 70 C3
Balfour Rd COW/LTMR OX4 ...... 52 B5
Ballard Cha ABGD OX14 ...... 67 H3
Baltic Whf OX/KTN OX1 ...... 40 B5
Bampton Cl COW/LTMR OX4 ...... 51 H5
Banbury Rd KID OX5 ...... 12 D2
OXN/BOT/CM OX2 ...... 2 C1
OXN/BOT/CM OX2 ...... 21 H5
OXN/BOT/CM OX2 ...... 32 A3
OXN/BOT/CM OX2 ...... 32 B5
WDSTK OX20 ...... 5 F2
Banjo Rd COW/LTMR OX4 ...... 51 H5
Bankside HEAD OX3 ...... 42 B2
KID OX5 ...... 12 D2
WIT/EY OX8 ...... 10 C3
Bannister Cl COW/LTMR OX4 ...... 50 D1
Bardwell Rd OXN/BOT/CM OX2 ...... 40 B1
Barfleur Cl ABGD OX14 ...... 68 A3
Barleycott La OX/KTN OX1 ...... 50 B4
Barlow Cl WHLY OX33 ...... 44 A5
Barn Cl KID OX5 ...... 13 E4
OXN/BOT/CM OX2 ...... 48 C2
Barnet St COW/LTMR OX4 ...... 51 F1
Barns Hay HEAD OX3 ...... 33 E4
Barn's Rd COW/LTMR OX4 ...... 51 G1
Barracks La COW/LTMR OX4 ...... 51 G1
Barrett St OXN/BOT/CM OX2 ...... 39 H5
Barrington Cl HEAD OX3 ...... 41 H3
WGFD OX10 ...... 77 F3
Barrow Hill Cl ABGD OX14 ...... 68 B4
Barrow Rd MCHM/KBPZ OX13 ...... 72 B1

Bartholomew Av KID OX5 ...... 20 C2
Bartholomew Cl WIT/EY OX8 ...... 28 A2
Bartholomew Rd
COW/LTMR OX4 ...... 51 H4
Bartlemas Cl COW/LTMR OX4 ...... 51 F1
Bartlemas Rd COW/LTMR OX4 ...... 51 F1
Barton La ABGD OX14 ...... 74 B2
HEAD OX3 ...... 42 A1
Barton Rd HEAD OX3 ...... 42 B1
Barton Village Rd HEAD OX3 ... 34 B5
Bassett Rd HEAD OX3 ...... 42 C1
Basset Wy KID OX5 ...... 13 G3
Bateman St HEAD OX3 ...... 41 H3
Bath Pl OX/KTN OX1 ...... 2 E5
Bath St ABGD OX14 ...... 73 C2
COW/LTMR OX4 ...... 3 J6
Bayswater Farm Rd HEAD OX3 ...... 42 D1
Bayswater Rd HEAD OX3 ...... 34 C5
HEAD OX3 ...... 42 D1
Beagle Cl ABGD OX14 ...... 68 B4
Beagles Cl KID OX5 ...... 13 H5
Bear Cl WDSTK OX20 ...... 5 E3
Bear La OX/KTN OX1 ...... 2 D6
Bears Hedge COW/LTMR OX4 ...... 51 F4
Beauchamp La COW/LTMR OX4 ...... 51 G4
Beaumont Buildings OX/KTN OX1 .. 2 B4
Beaumont La OX/KTN OX1 ...... 2 C4
Beaumont Pl OX/KTN OX1 ...... 2 C4
Beaumont Rd HEAD OX3 ...... 42 B2
Beaumont St OX/KTN OX1 ...... 2 A6
Becket St OX/KTN OX1 ...... 2 A6
Becketts Cl WIT/EY OX8 ...... 9 G3
Beckley Ct HEAD OX3 ...... 25 E5
Bedford St COW/LTMR OX4 ...... 51 E2
Bedwells Heath OX/KTN OX1 ...... 59 E2
Beech Cl MCHM/KBPZ OX13 ...... 58 B4
Beech Crs KID OX5 ...... 21 F1
Beech Croft Rd
OXN/BOT/CM OX2 ...... 32 A4
The Beeches HEAD OX3 ...... 42 B1
Beechey Av HEAD OX3 ...... 41 E1
Beech Rd HEAD OX3 ...... 41 H2
OXN/BOT/CM OX2 ...... 49 E1
WHLY OX33 ...... 54 C1
WIT/EY OX8 ...... 28 B2
Beef La OX/KTN OX1 ...... 2 C6
Begbroke Crs KID OX5 ...... 12 B3
Belbroughton Rd
OXN/BOT/CM OX2 ...... 32 A5
Belgrove Cl KID OX5 ...... 13 E4
Bell Cl WIT/EY OX8 ...... 19 C5
Bellenger Wy KID OX5 ...... 13 E4
Bell La WHLY OX33 ...... 44 C5
WIT/EY OX8 ...... 19 C5
Belvedere Rd COW/LTMR OX4 ...... 51 F1
Ben Cl KID OX5 ...... 13 F3
Benmead Rd KID OX5 ...... 13 F3
Benson Pl OXN/BOT/CM OX2 ...... 40 C1
Benson Rd ABGD OX14 ...... 67 F4
HEAD OX3 ...... 42 A5
Bergamont Pl COW/LTMR OX4 .. 62 B2
Bergen Av ABGD OX14 ...... 73 E5
Berkeley Rd OX/KTN OX1 ...... 59 F2
Bernard Cl KID OX5 ...... 20 D2
Bernwood Rd HEAD OX3 ...... 42 B1
Berry Cl COW/LTMR OX4 ...... 52 C5
Berry Cft ABGD OX14 ...... 67 F5
Berrymere Rd MCHM/KBPZ OX13 .. 58 B4
Bertie Pl OX/KTN OX1 ...... 50 C3
Bertie Rd OXN/BOT/CM OX2 ...... 48 A3
Besselsleigh Rd
MCHM/KBPZ OX13 ...... 57 H3
Betty La OX/KTN OX1 ...... 50 B5
Between Towns Rd
COW/LTMR OX4 ...... 51 H3
Beverley Cl ABGD OX14 ...... 67 F5
Bevington Rd OXN/BOT/CM OX2 ... 2 B1
Bhandari Cl COW/LTMR OX4 ...... 51 C2
Bicester Rd KID OX5 ...... 13 H5

Bickerton Rd HEAD OX3 ...... 41 H3
Binsey La OXN/BOT/CM OX2 ...... 39 F3
Binswood Av HEAD OX3 ...... 42 B3
Birchfield Cl COW/LTMR OX4 ...... 62 B1
Birch Rd STAD OX44 ...... 63 G1
Birchwood Dr KID OX5 ...... 6 C3
Biscoe Ct WHLY OX33 ...... 44 D5
Bishop Kirk Pl OXN/BOT/CM OX2 .. 31 H3
Bitterell WIT/EY OX8 ...... 28 B3
Blackberry La STAD OX44 ...... 62 D3
Blackbird Leys Rd
COW/LTMR OX4 ...... 52 A5
COW/LTMR OX4 ...... 52 B5
Blackfriars Rd OX/KTN OX1 ...... 40 B5
Blackhall Rd OX/KTN OX1 ...... 2 C3
Blacklands Wy ABGD OX14 ...... 72 D2
Blackman Cl OX/KTN OX1 ...... 60 D1
Blacknall Rd ABGD OX14 ...... 73 F3
Blacksmiths Meadow
COW/LTMR OX4 ...... 62 C2
Blackstock Cl HEAD OX3 ...... 52 B1
Blackthorn Cl HEAD OX3 ...... 42 A1
Bladon Cl OXN/BOT/CM OX2 ...... 31 G2
Bladon Rd WDSTK OX20 ...... 5 G5
Blandford Av OXN/BOT/CM OX2 ...... 31 H1
Blandford Rd KID OX5 ...... 13 E2
Blankstone Cl WIT/EY OX8 ...... 28 A3
Blay Cl COW/LTMR OX4 ...... 52 B5
Blenheim Dr OXN/BOT/CM OX2 ... 31 H2
Blenheim La WIT/EY OX8 ...... 17 F1
Blenheim Rd KID OX5 ...... 13 G4
STAD OX44 ...... 65 H5
WHLY OX33 ...... 53 F1
Blenheim Wy WHLY OX33 ...... 53 F1
Bletchingdon Rd KID OX5 ...... 7 H5
KID OX5 ...... 14 D1
Blomfield Pl OXN/BOT/CM OX2 .. 2 A2
Blossoms Gld ABGD OX14 ...... 60 D5
The Blowings WIT/EY OX8 ...... 9 F5
Bluebell Ct COW/LTMR OX4 ...... 62 C2
Bluebell Ride ABGD OX14 ...... 60 D4
Blue Boar St OX/KTN OX1 ...... 2 D6
Bobby Fryer Cl
COW/LTMR OX4 ...... 52 B4
Boddington La WIT/EY OX8 ...... 8 B4
Bodley Rd COW/LTMR OX4 ...... 51 H5
Bolsover Cl WIT/EY OX8 ...... 9 F3
Bolton's La WIT/EY OX8 ...... 9 H1
Bonar Rd HEAD OX3 ...... 42 B4
Boreford Rd ABGD OX14 ...... 68 A4
Borough Wk ABGD OX14 ...... 67 F5
Borrowmead Rd HEAD OX3 ...... 33 G5
Bostock Rd ABGD OX14 ...... 73 E2
Boswell Rd COW/LTMR OX4 ...... 51 H4
Botley Rd OXN/BOT/CM OX2 ...... 39 H4
The Boulevard KID OX5 ...... 12 C2
Boulter Dr ABGD OX14 ...... 67 H3
Boulter St COW/LTMR OX4 ...... 3 H6
Boults Cl HEAD OX3 ...... 33 E5
Boults La HEAD OX3 ...... 33 E5
Boundary Brook Rd
COW/LTMR OX4 ...... 51 F2
Boundary Cl WDSTK OX20 ...... 5 E3
Bourlon Wd ABGD OX14 ...... 67 E5
Bourne Cl OXN/BOT/CM OX2 ...... 32 A1
Bowerman Cl KID OX5 ...... 13 E4
Bowgrave Copse ABGD OX14 ...... 68 B5
Bowness Av HEAD OX3 ...... 41 F1
Bowyer Rd ABGD OX14 ...... 73 G1
Boxhill Rd ABGD OX14 ...... 73 G1
Boxhill Wk ABGD OX14 ...... 73 F1
Boxwell Cl ABGD OX14 ...... 68 A4
Bracegirdle Rd HEAD OX3 ...... 42 B4
Bradmore Rd OXN/BOT/CM OX2 ... 40 B1
Brake Hl COW/LTMR OX4 ...... 62 D2
Brambling Wy COW/LTMR OX4 .. 62 A1
Brampton Cl ABGD OX14 ...... 67 F5
Brampton Rd HEAD OX3 ...... 42 B1

D

ank ABGD OX14 .... 74 A1
OX/KTN OX1 .... 40 A5
s Rd OXN/LTMR OX4 .. 51 F5
a MCHM/KBPZ OX13 .. 67 F1
nd MCHM/KBPZ OX13 .. 66 D3
ood Av KID OX5 .... 20 C2
ard Av COW/LTMR OX4 .. 51 F5
ny Rd COW/LTMR OX4 .. 51 E2
a La COW/LTMR OX4 .. 31 H2
Nicholls CI COW/LTMR OX4 .. 61 C1
Walter CI
/BOT/CM OX2 .... 32 A1
n PI OXN/BOT/CM OX2 .. 39 H3
n St COW/LTMR OX4 .... 3 H7
ourt Rd OXN/BOT/CM OX2.. 48 C1
eld Rd
/BOT/CM OX2 .... 38 C4
bbey CI ABGD OX14 .... 67 F4
rt CI KID OX5 .... 13 F3
are Wy OXN/BOT/CM OX2.. 43 E1
h Av HEAD OX3 .... 43 E1
d OX3 .... 42 A5
an's La OXN/BOT/CM OX2.. 47 H3
ark St COW/LTMR OX4 .. 41 E5
n CI ABGD OX14 .... 74 A1
/BOT/CM OX2 .... 38 B5
n HI STAD OX44 .... 64 C2
n La STAD OX44 .... 63 H2
CI HEAD OX3 .... 33 F5
nt Av HEAD OX3 .... 41 F1
ant CI MCHM/KBPZ OX13 ... 66 D4
rough Crs COW/LTMR OX4.. 51 E5
sne Furze HEAD OX3 .... 41 H4
eux PI COW/LTMR OX4 .. 51 F5
nd PI OXN/BOT/CM OX2.. 32 A4
y Rd COW/LTMR OX4 .. 41 F5
on Rd COW/LTMR OX4 .. 51 H4
n Ct ABGD OX14 .... 73 C2
oscoe CI COW/LTMR OX4.. 52 A2
gton Bridge Rd
/LTMR OX4 .... 51 E3
uart PI COW/LTMR OX4 .. 51 C1
arr CI HEAD OX3 .... 33 F5
ester CI HEAD OX3 .... 42 C4
ester Crs HEAD OX3 .... 67 H5
Mouse CI
/BOT/CM OX2 .... 31 G2
ouse CI WIT/EY OX8 .... 28 C2
side End HEAD OX3 .... 42 D2
side Rd HEAD OX3 .... 42 C2
r Rd OXN/BOT/CM OX2.. 39 H5
n East Wy ABGD OX14 .. 78 D4
n Rd ABGD OX14 .... 78 D1
.... 79 E3
Acre Rd COW/LTMR OX4 .. 51 F1
Wy COW/LTMR OX4 .... 52 C5
le CI ABGD OX14.... 68 D4
on Dr COW/LTMR OX4 .. 61 C1
d CI ABGD OX14 .... 68 A4
.... 13 C4
st OXN/BOT/CM OX2 .. 39 G4
n CI WIT/EY OX8 .... 28 A2
.... 74 A1
re Rd ABGD OX14 .... 67 H3
ck Wy COW/LTMR OX4 .. 62 B2
n Rd HEAD OX3 .... 41 H1
m PI OX3 .... 42 A4

E

OXN/BOT/CM OX2 .... 39 G4
Dr ABGD OX14 .... 68 B5
COW/LTMR OX4 .... 41 F5
urch COW/LTMR OX4 .. 51 E5
n Av COW/LTMR OX4 .. 51 C5
n By-pass Rd
/LTMR OX4 .... 51 H5
n Rd OX1 .... 61 F1
OX3 .... 42 C2
eld CI COW/LTMR OX4 .. 52 B1
aint Helen St
OX14 .... 73 C2
OXN/BOT/CM OX2 .. 39 H4
OX3 .... 78 C4
Rd MCHM/KBPZ OX13 .. 57 E1
ft ABGD OX14 .... 67 H4
r HEAD OX3 .... 41 F1
ombe Rd HEAD OX3 .... 3 H1
way Rd HEAD OX3 .... 31 H1
OX3 .... 40 D1
urgh Dr KID OX5 .... 13 H4
rd OX/KTN OX1 .... 50 B2

Edmund Halley Rd
COW/LTMR OX4.... 61 G2
Edmund Rd COW/LTMR OX4 .. 51 H5
Edward Rd OX/KTN OX1 .... 60 D2
Edward St ABGD OX14 .... 73 E2
Egerton Rd COW/LTMR OX4 .. 51 F4
Eighth Av HEAD OX3 .... 42 C5
Elder Wy COW/LTMR OX4 .. 62 C2
Eldridge CI ABGD OX14 .... 67 G4
Eleanor CI COW/LTMR OX4 .. 51 G4
Electric Av OXN/BOT/CM OX2 .. 39 H5
Elizabeth Av ABGD OX14.... 68 B4
Ellesmere Rd COW/LTMR OX4 .. 51 F4
Elm CI WHLY OX33 .... 54 D1
Elm Dr STAD OX44 .... 63 F1
Elm Gv KID OX5 .... 21 G1
Elms Dr HEAD OX3 .... 33 E5
Elms Pde OXN/BOT/CM OX2 .. 39 E4
Elms Rd OXN/BOT/CM OX2.... 38 D4
WIT/EY OX8 .... 19 F5
Elmthorpe Rd OXN/BOT/CM OX2 .. 31 F2
Elm Tree CI ABGD OX14 .... 51 G5
Elm Tree Wk MCHM/KBPZ OX13 .. 66 C5
Elsfield Rd HEAD OX3 .... 33 E4
Elsfield Wy OXN/BOT/CM OX2 .. 32 A1
Elton Crs WHLY OX33.... 54 D1
Elwes CI ABGD OX14 .... 74 A1
Ely CI ABGD OX14 .... 72 D3
Emperor Gdns COW/LTMR OX4 .. 62 B2
Eney CI ABGD OX14 .... 68 B4
Erica CI COW/LTMR OX4 .. 62 C1
Essex St COW/LTMR OX4 .. 51 F1
Ethelred Ct HEAD OX3 .... 41 H1
Evans CI WIT/EY OX8 .... 28 B2
Evans CI KID OX5 .... 13 G4
Evans La KID OX5 .... 13 G4
Evans Rd WIT/EY OX8 .... 28 B3
Evelin Rd ABGD OX14 .... 67 F5
Evelyn CI OXN/BOT/CM OX2.... 38 C5
Evenlode Crs KID OX5 .... 12 B2
Evenlode Dr WGFD OX10 .... 77 F3
WIT/EY OX8 .... 9 F3
Evenlode Pk ABGD OX14 .... 68 A5
Everard CI HEAD OX3 .... 42 A4
Ewert PI OXN/BOT/CM OX2 .. 32 A4
Ewin CI HEAD OX3 .... 33 E5
Exbourne Rd ABGD OX14 .... 73 E2
Exeter Rd KID OX5 .... 13 F3
Eynsham Rd OXN/BOT/CM OX2 .. 37 G3
WIT/EY OX8 .... 29 F1
Eyot PI OXN/BOT/CM OX2 .. 51 E1
Eyston Wy ABGD OX14 .... 72 D2

F

Faber CI COW/LTMR OX4.... 61 H1
Fairacres ABGD OX14 .... 72 C2
Fairacres Rd COW/LTMR OX4.... 51 E2
Fairfax Av HEAD OX3 .... 40 D1
Fairfax Rd COW/LTMR OX4 .. 52 B2
KID OX5 .... 21 G1
Fairfield PI ABGD OX14 .... 73 C1
Fairlawn End OXN/BOT/CM OX2 .. 31 G2
Fairlie Rd COW/LTMR OX4 .. 51 C5
Fair Vw HEAD OX3 .... 52 A1
Falcon CI COW/LTMR OX4 .. 62 A1
Falstaff CI WIT/EY OX8 .... 28 A2
Fane Dr WGFD OX10 .... 77 F3
Fane Rd HEAD OX3 .... 32 D5
Fanshawe PI COW/LTMR OX4 ... 52 B3
Faringdon Rd ABGD OX14 .... 73 F1
MCHM/KBPZ OX13 .... 66 A5
OXN/BOT/CM OX2.... 47 H5
Farm CI COW/LTMR OX4 .. 62 C2
KID OX5 .... 13 F3
Farm Close La WHLY OX33.... 44 C5
Farm Close Rd WHLY OX33.... 44 C5
Farmer PI HEAD OX3 .... 41 E1
Farmoor Ct OXN/BOT/CM OX2 .. 37 F3
Farm Rd ABGD OX14 .... 67 G4
Farndon Rd OXN/BOT/CM OX2 .... 40 A1
Faulkner St OX/KTN OX1 .... 2 C7
Feilden Gv HEAD OX3 .... 41 F2
Fenlock Rd WIT/EY OX8 .... 10 C3
Fennel Wy ABGD OX14 .... 74 B1
Ferguson PI ABGD OX14 .... 74 B1
Fernhill CI KID OX5 .... 13 E4
Fern Hill Rd COW/LTMR OX4 .. 52 A3
Fernhill Rd KID OX5 .... 12 B4
Ferny CI ABGD OX14 .... 68 D3
Ferry Hinksey Rd
OX3 .... 39 H4
Ferry Pool Rd OXN/BOT/CM OX2 .. 32 A4
Ferry Rd HEAD OX3 .... 3 J2
Ferry Wk ABGD OX14 .... 73 G4

Fettiplace CI MCHM/KBPZ OX13 .... 56 D4
Fettiplace Rd HEAD OX3.... 34 B5
Field Av COW/LTMR OX4 .... 62 C2
Field CI KID OX5 .... 13 G4
KID OX5 .... 20 C1
Fieldfare Rd COW/LTMR OX4 .. 62 B3
Field House Dr OXN/BOT/CM OX2.. 31 H2
Fieldside ABGD OX14.... 67 H5
ABGD OX14 .... 81 H4
The Field MCHM/KBPZ OX13 .. 58 A5
Fiennes Rd COW/LTMR OX4 .. 51 H5
Finch CI HEAD OX3 .... 41 H3
Finmore CI ABGD OX14 .... 73 F1
Finmore Rd OXN/BOT/CM OX2 .. 39 E5
Firs Meadow COW/LTMR OX4 .. 62 B3
First Av HEAD OX3 .... 42 C5
First Turn OXN/BOT/CM OX2 .. 31 G2
Fir Trees OX/KTN OX1 .... 60 D4
Fisher CI ABGD OX14 .... 78 B3
Fitzharry's Rd ABGD OX14 .... 73 G1
Fitzherbert CI COW/LTMR OX4 .. 51 E4
Five Mile Dr OXN/BOT/CM OX2 .. 31 H1
Flatford PI KID OX5 .... 12 D2
Flaxfield Rd COW/LTMR OX4 .. 62 C1
Flemings Rd WDSTK OX20 .... 5 F3
Fletcher CI KID OX5 .... 20 C2
Fletcher Rd COW/LTMR OX4 .. 52 B2
Flexney PI HEAD OX3 .... 42 A4
Florence CI KID OX5.... 13 F4
Florence Park Rd
COW/LTMR OX4.... 51 G3
Floyd's Rw OX/KTN OX1 .... 2 D7
Fogwell Rd OXN/BOT/CM OX2.... 38 B5
Folly Br OX/KTN OX1 .... 40 B5
Fords CI WHLY OX33 .... 53 F2
Forest Rd HEAD OX3 .... 42 C2
Forest Side OX/KTN OX1.... 50 C5
Forget-me-not Wy
COW/LTMR OX4 .... 62 B2
Forster La OXN/BOT/CM OX2 .. 47 H4
The Forties STAD OX44 .... 65 H1
Fortnam CI HEAD OX3 .... 41 G2
Foster Rd ABGD OX14 .... 67 G3
Fourth Av HEAD OX3 .... 42 C5
Foxborough Rd ABGD OX14 .... 68 D4
Fox CI STAD OX44 .... 63 C1
Foxcombe La OX/KTN OX1 .. 59 H3
Foxcombe Rd OX/KTN OX1 .. 59 H2
Fox Crs OX/KTN OX1 .... 50 D3
Foxdown CI KID OX5 .... 13 F3
Fox Furlong COW/LTMR OX4 .. 61 F2
Foxglove CI COW/LTMR OX4 .. 62 B2
Foxglove Rd KID OX5 .... 12 C4
Fox La MCHM/KBPZ OX13 .... 58 D5
Foxton CI OXN/BOT/CM OX2 .. 31 G1
Foxwell Dr HEAD OX3 .... 33 C5
Francis Little Dr ABGD OX14 .. 73 E4
Franklin CI KID OX5 .... 13 G3
Franklin Rd HEAD OX3 .... 41 C2
Franklyn CI ABGD OX14 .... 72 D3
Frederick Rd COW/LTMR OX4 .. 52 A4
Freeborn CI KID OX5 .... 13 F2
Freelands Rd COW/LTMR OX4 .. 51 E3
Frenchay Rd OXN/BOT/CM OX2 .. 31 H3
Friars Whf OX/KTN OX1 .... 40 B5
Friday La WHLY OX33 .... 44 C5
Frilsham St ABGD OX14 .... 79 H5
Fruitlands WIT/EY OX8 .... 27 H2
Frys HI COW/LTMR OX4 .... 62 C1
Fullwell CI ABGD OX14.... 67 F5
Furlong CI COW/LTMR OX4.... 52 A3
Fyfield Rd OXN/BOT/CM OX2.... 40 B1

G

Gainsborough Gn ABGD OX14 .. 73 E4
Gaisford Rd COW/LTMR OX4 .. 51 H4
Gall CI ABGD OX14 .... 74 B1
Galley Fld ABGD OX14 .... 74 A1
Galpin CI COW/LTMR OX4 .. 51 F1
The Gardens ABGD OX14 .... 68 D3
Gardiner CI ABGD OX14 .... 74 B1
WHLY OX33 .... 44 B4
Gardiner St HEAD OX3.... 42 A3
Garford CI ABGD OX14 .... 68 A4
Garford Rd OXN/BOT/CM OX2 .. 32 B5
Garsington Rd COW/LTMR OX4 .. 52 A3
The Garth KID OX5 .... 20 C2
OXN/BOT/CM OX2 .. 39 E5
Gathorne Rd HEAD OX3.... 42 A3
Gentian Rd COW/LTMR OX4 .. 62 C1
Geoffrey Barbour Rd ABGD OX14.. 73 G1
George Moore CI COW/LTMR OX4 .. 51 F2
George St OX/KTN OX1 .... 2 B5
George Street Ms OX/KTN OX1 .... 2 B5
Gerard PI COW/LTMR OX4 .... 51 H3

Gibbs Crs OXN/BOT/CM OX2 .... 39 H5
Gibson CI ABGD OX14 .... 67 H3
Gidley Wy WHLY OX33 .... 53 H1
Giles CI COW/LTMR OX4.... 61 G1
Giles Rd COW/LTMR OX4 .... 61 G1
Gillians Wy COW/LTMR OX4 .. 51 G2
Ginge CI ABGD OX14 .... 68 A4
Gipsy La HEAD OX3 .... 41 G3
Girdlestone Rd HEAD OX3 .... 42 A4
Gladstone Rd HEAD OX3 .... 42 B2
Glanville Rd COW/LTMR OX4 .. 51 G1
Glebelands HEAD OX3 .... 42 A5
Glebe Rd OXN/BOT/CM OX2 .... 47 H3
Glebe St COW/LTMR OX4 .... 3 J6
The Glebe ABGD OX14 .... 80 A1
OXN/BOT/CM OX2.... 47 H3
WHLY OX33 .... 44 C5
Gloucester La OX/KTN OX1 .... 2 C5
Gloucester St OX/KTN OX1 .... 2 C5
Glovers CI WDSTK OX20.... 5 F3
Glyme CI ABGD OX14 .... 68 A5
WDSTK OX20 .... 5 E2
Glyme Dr WGFD OX10 .... 77 G3
Glyme Wy WIT/EY OX8 .... 9 G4
Godfrey CI ABGD OX14 .... 73 F3
Godstow Rd OXN/BOT/CM OX2.... 30 D3
Godwyn CI ABGD OX14 .... 73 F1
Golafre Rd ABGD OX14 .... 73 F4
Golden Rd COW/LTMR OX4 .. 51 F1
Gold St STAD OX44 .... 65 G5
Gooseacre ABGD OX14 .... 68 D4
Gordon CI HEAD OX3 .... 33 E5
Gordon Dr ABGD OX14 .... 68 B5
Gordon St OX/KTN OX1.... 50 B2
Gorse Leas HEAD OX3 .... 33 G5
Gosford CI KID OX5 .... 21 G1
Goslyn CI HEAD OX3 .... 42 A4
Gouldland Gdns HEAD OX3 .... 41 G1
Grand Br WDSTK OX20 .... 4 C4
Grange CI OXN/BOT/CM OX2 .. 38 C4
Grange Rd COW/LTMR OX4 .. 61 G1
Grants Ms COW/LTMR OX4 .... 3 J7
The Grates COW/LTMR OX4 .. 51 H4
Gravel La ABGD OX14 .... 78 C4
Gravel Pits La KID OX5 .... 20 C1
Grays Rd HEAD OX3 .... 41 G3
Great Clarendon St
OXN/BOT/CM OX2 .... 2 A3
Great Close Rd KID OX5 .... 20 C2
Great Md OXN/BOT/CM OX2 .... 2 A5
Crebe CI ABGD OX14 .... 73 G4
Greenacres ABGD OX14 .... 78 C4
Green Close Goose
OXN/BOT/CM OX2 .... 31 F2
Greenfinch CI COW/LTMR OX4.... 62 C2
Green Furlong WGFD OX10 .... 77 F4
Green HI COW/LTMR OX4 .... 62 D1
Green La MCHM/KBPZ OX13 .. 59 H5
MCHM/KBPZ OX13 .... 66 B1
OXN/BOT/CM OX2.... 38 B5
WDSTK OX20 .... 5 E2
Green PI OX/KTN OX1 .... 50 C2
Green Ridges HEAD OX3 .... 42 D1
Green Rd HEAD OX3 .... 42 C2
KID OX5 .... 13 F4
Green's Rd WIT/EY OX8.... 28 B2
Green St COW/LTMR OX4 .... 41 F5
The Green STAD OX44 .... 54 C5
STAD OX44 .... 63 H2
WDSTK OX20 .... 11 E2
WIT/EY OX8 .... 8 C2
WIT/EY OX8 .... 19 F5
Grenoble Rd COW/LTMR OX4.... 61 G3
COW/LTMR OX4.... 62 D2
Greystones Ct KID OX5 .... 13 E3
Grosvenor Rd OXN/BOT/CM OX2 .. 49 F2
Grovelands KID OX5 .... 13 E4
Grovelands Rd HEAD OX3 .... 42 D3
Grove Rd WDSTK OX20 .... 11 F1
Grove St OXN/BOT/CM OX2 .. 32 A3
The Grove ABGD OX14 .... 68 A4
Grundy CI ABGD OX14 .... 74 A1
Grundy Crs OX/KTN OX1 .... 60 D3
Grunsell CI HEAD OX3 .... 33 G5
Gurden PI HEAD OX3 .... 42 B1
Gurl CI HEAD OX3 .... 42 B1
Gwyneth Rd COW/LTMR OX4.... 61 F1

H

Hadland Rd ABGD OX14 .... 74 B1
Hadow Rd HEAD OX3 .... 41 F1
Haldane Rd COW/LTMR OX4 .... 52 C5
Halliday HI HEAD OX3 .... 33 G5
Halls CI ABGD OX14 .... 78 D3
OXN/BOT/CM OX2.... 48 D1

Hamble Dr *ABGD* OX14 .... 68 A5
Hamels La *OX/KTN* OX1 .... 59 G2
The Hamel *OX/KTN* OX1 .... 2 B6 ▉
Hamilton Rd *OXN/BOT/CM* OX2 .... 32 A3
Hampden Dr *KID* OX5 .... 21 G1
Hampden Rd *COW/LTMR* OX4 .... 51 H4
Hanborough Cl *WIT/EY* OX8 .... 28 B2
Hanborough Rd *WIT/EY* OX8 .... 28 B2
Handlo Pl *HEAD* OX3 .... 42 C1 ▉
Hanson Rd *ABGD* OX14 .... 67 G3
Harberton Md *ABGD* 3 K2
Harbord Rd *OXN/BOT/CM* OX2 .... 21 H5
Harcourt Hl *OXN/BOT/CM* OX2 .... 49 E3
Harcourt Ter *HEAD* OX3 .... 41 G3
Harcourt Wy *ABGD* OX14 .... 67 G5
Harding Rd *ABGD* OX14 .... 73 E1
Hardings Cl *COW/LTMR* OX4 .... 51 G5 ▉
Hardwick Av *KID* OX5 .... 13 F5
Harebell Rd *COW/LTMR* OX4 .... 62 C1
Harefields *OXN/BOT/CM* OX2 .... 32 A1
Harley Rd *OXN/BOT/CM* OX2 .... 39 G4
Harlow Wy *HEAD* OX3 .... 33 E3
Harolde Cl *HEAD* OX3 .... 42 A1
Harold Hicks Pl *COW/LTMR* OX4 .... 51 E2 ▉
Harold White Cl *HEAD* OX3 .... 42 C3 ▉
Harpes Rd *OXN/BOT/CM* OX2 .... 32 A2
Harpsichord Pl *COW/LTMR* OX4 .. 3 J6 ▉
Harrison's La *WDSTK* OX20 .... 4 D3 ▉
Harrow Rd *COW/LTMR* OX4 .... 52 C5
Hart Cl *ABGD* OX14 .... 74 B1
Harts Cl *KID* OX5 .... 13 E4
Hart St *OXN/BOT/CM* OX2 .... 2 A3 ▉
Harwell Cl *ABGD* OX14 .... 67 H5 ▉
Haseley Rd *STAD* OX44 .... 65 G5
Hathaways *WHLY* OX33 .... 44 C5 ▉
Havelock Rd *COW/LTMR* OX4 .... 51 H3
Hawkins Ct *OXN/BOT/CM* OX2 .... 51 E2 ▉
Hawkins Wy *MCHM/KBPZ* OX13 .. 58 C5
Hawksmoor Rd
 OXN/BOT/CM OX2 .... 32 A1
Hawkswell Gdns
 OXN/BOT/CM OX2 .... 32 B3
Hawthorn Av *HEAD* OX3 .... 42 A2
Hawthorne Av
 MCHM/KBPZ OX13 .... 66 C5
Hawthorne Cl
 OXN/BOT/CM OX2 .... 39 E5 ▉
Hawthorn Rd *WIT/EY* OX8 .... 28 B2
Hawthorn Wy *KID* OX5 .... 13 F5 ▉
Hayes Cl *HEAD* OX3 .... 3 J1
Hayfield Rd *OXN/BOT/CM* OX2 .... 32 A5
Haynes Rd *HEAD* OX3 .... 32 D5
Hayward Rd *OXN/BOT/CM* OX2 .... 21 H5
Haywards Rd *ABGD* OX14 .... 78 C4
Hazel Crs *KID* OX5 .... 21 F1
Hazelnut Pth *ABGD* OX14 .... 60 D4 ▉
Hazel Rd *OXN/BOT/CM* OX2 .... 38 D4
Headington Rd *HEAD* OX3 .... 3 K5
Headley Wy *HEAD* OX3 .... 41 G2
Healey Cl *ABGD* OX14 .... 73 F3
Hean Cl *ABGD* OX14 .... 68 A4
Heath Cl *HEAD* OX3 .... 42 A5
Heathcote Pl *ABGD* OX14 .... 68 B5 ▉
Heather Pl *HEAD* OX3 .... 41 E1
Heath La *WDSTK* OX20 .... 11 E2
Hedge End *WDSTK* OX20 .... 5 F4
Hedgemead Av *ABGD* OX14 .... 68 B5
Helen Rd *OXN/BOT/CM* OX2 .... 39 G4
Helwys Rd *KID* OX5 .... 13 F2
Hendred St *COW/LTMR* OX4 .... 51 G3
Hendred Wy *ABGD* OX14 .... 68 A5
Hengrove Cl *HEAD* OX3 .... 42 A1
Henley Av *COW/LTMR* OX4 .... 51 F3
Henley Rd *COW/LTMR* OX4 .... 61 G3
Henleys La *ABGD* OX14 .... 78 C3
Henley St *COW/LTMR* OX4 .... 51 E1
Henor Mill Cl *ABGD* OX14 .... 68 A4 ▉
Henry Rd *OXN/BOT/CM* OX2 .... 39 H4
Henry Taunt Cl *HEAD* OX3 .... 34 B5
Hensington Cl *WDSTK* OX20 .... 5 F3
Hensington Rd *WDSTK* OX20 .... 5 E3
Henwood Dr *OX/KTN* OX1 .... 58 B2
Herbert Cl *ABGD* OX14 .... 51 G1
Herman Cl *ABGD* OX14 .... 74 A1
Hermitage Rd *ABGD* OX14 .... 73 E3
Hernes Rd *OXN/BOT/CM* OX2 .... 32 A5
Heron Ct *ABGD* OX14 .... 73 G5
Heron's Wk *ABGD* OX14 .... 67 G5
Herschel Crs *COW/LTMR* OX4 .... 51 H5
Hertford St *COW/LTMR* OX4 .... 51 F1
Heycroft *WIT/EY* OX8 .... 28 B3
Heyford Hill La *COW/LTMR* OX4 .... 61 E1
Heyford Md *KID* OX5 .... 13 E3 ▉
Hid's Copse Rd
 OXN/BOT/CM OX2 .... 48 B1
High Cross Wy *HEAD* OX3 .... 34 B5 ▉
Highfield Av *HEAD* OX3 .... 41 H3
High St *ABGD* OX14 .... 73 G2

ABGD OX14 .... 78 D3
ABGD OX14 .... 81 H1
HEAD OX3 .... 24 D4
KID OX5 .... 13 F3
KID OX5 .... 15 E3
OX/KTN OX1 .... 2 E5
OXN/BOT/CM OX2 .... 47 G3
STAD OX44 .... 64 C1
WDSTK OX20 .... 4 D3
WHLY OX33 .... 44 B5
WIT/EY OX8 .... 28 B3
Hillary Wy *WHLY* OX33 .... 54 D1
Hillcraft Rd *WHLY* OX33 .... 35 G3
Hilliat Flds *ABGD* OX14 .... 78 C3
Hilliers Cl *ABGD* OX14 .... 79 G4
Hill Ri *WDSTK* OX20 .... 4 D1
 WHLY OX33 .... 53 G2
Hillsborough Rd *COW/LTMR* OX4 .. 51 H4
Hillside *OXN/BOT/CM* OX2 .... 48 B2
The Hill *STAD* OX44 .... 63 H2
Hilltop Gdns *HEAD* OX3 .... 15 E3
Hill Top Rd *COW/LTMR* OX4 .... 41 G5
Hill Vw *HEAD* OX3 .... 42 D1
Hill View La *MCHM/KBPZ* OX13 ... 58 B3
Hillview Rd *ABGD* OX14 .... 67 G4
 OXN/BOT/CM OX2 .... 39 H4
Hinksey Hl *OX/KTN* OX1 .... 50 A5
Hobbs Cl *ABGD* OX14 .... 74 A1 ▉
Hobby Ct *COW/LTMR* OX4 .... 62 C2 ▉
Hobbyhorse La *ABGD* OX14 .... 80 A5
Hobson Rd *OXN/BOT/CM* OX2 .... 32 A3
Hockmore St *COW/LTMR* OX4 .... 51 H4
Hodges Ct *OX/KTN* OX1 .... 50 B1 ▉
Hogarth Pl *ABGD* OX14 .... 73 F4
Holland Pl *HEAD* OX3 .... 42 B5 ▉
Holley Crs *HEAD* OX3 .... 42 A2
Holloway Rd *WHLY* OX33 .... 44 C5
Hollow Furlong *WIT/EY* OX8 .... 19 F5
Hollow Wy *COW/LTMR* OX4 .... 52 A2 ▉
Hollybush Rw *OX/KTN* OX1 .... 2 A6
The Holt *ABGD* OX14 .... 73 H1
Holy Cl *KID* OX5 .... 13 F5
Holyoake Rd *HEAD* OX3 .... 42 A2
Holywell Cl *ABGD* OX14 .... 68 B4 ▉
Holywell St *OX/KTN* OX1 .... 2 E4
Home Cl *KID* OX5 .... 13 F3
 MCHM/KBPZ OX13 .... 58 C4
 OXN/BOT/CM OX2 .... 31 E2
Homestall Cl *OXN/BOT/CM* OX2 .. 38 C4
The Homestead *KID* OX5 .... 13 E4 ▉
 WDSTK OX20 .... 11 F1
Honeybottom La
 MCHM/KBPZ OX13 .... 66 A2
Honeysuckle Gv
 COW/LTMR OX4 .... 62 D1 ▉
Honor Cl *KID* OX5 .... 13 G4
Hornbeam Dr *COW/LTMR* OX4 .. 62 D1 ▉
Horseman Cl *HEAD* OX3 .... 33 E5
Horsemere La *WIT/EY* OX8 .... 19 G5
Horspath Driftway *HEAD* OX3 .... 52 B1
Horspath Rd *COW/LTMR* OX4 .... 52 C2
Horwood Cl *HEAD* OX3 .... 41 H2 ▉
Hosker Cl *HEAD* OX3 .... 42 D1
Hound Cl *ABGD* OX14 .... 68 B4
Howard St *COW/LTMR* OX4 .... 51 E2
Howe Cl *WHLY* OX33 .... 44 B5
Hugh Allen Crs *HEAD* OX3 .... 3 J1
Humfrey Rd *HEAD* OX3 .... 42 C1
Hundred Acres Cl *HEAD* OX3 .... 52 B1
Hunsdon Rd *COW/LTMR* OX4 .... 51 F4
Hunter Cl *ABGD* OX14 .... 68 A3
 COW/LTMR OX4 .... 52 B2
Hurdeswell *WIT/EY* OX8 .... 9 G3 ▉
Hurst La *OXN/BOT/CM* OX2 .... 48 C2
 WIT/EY OX8 .... 17 F1
Hurst Rise Rd *OXN/BOT/CM* OX2 .. 38 D5
Hurst St *COW/LTMR* OX4 .... 51 E1
Hutchcombe Farm Cl
 OXN/BOT/CM OX2 .... 48 D1 ▉
Hutchcomb Rd
 OXN/BOT/CM OX2 .... 38 D5
Huxley Cl *MCHM/KBPZ* OX13 .... 58 C5
Hyacinth Wk *COW/LTMR* OX4 .. 62 B3 ▉
The Hyde *ABGD* OX14 .... 73 E4
Hythe Bridge St *OX/KTN* OX1 .. 2 A5 ▉

I

Iffley Rd *COW/LTMR* OX4 .... 51 E1
Iffley Turn *COW/LTMR* OX4 .... 51 F3
Ilsley Rd *HEAD* OX3 .... 42 B1
Ingle Cl *HEAD* OX3 .... 41 G1
Inkerman Cl *ABGD* OX14 .... 67 E5
Inott Furze *HEAD* OX3 .... 52 A1
Isis Cl *ABGD* OX14 .... 68 A5
 WIT/EY OX8 .... 9 G4

Islip Rd *KID* OX5 .... 7 H1
 OXN/BOT/CM OX2 .... 32 A2

J

Jack Argent Cl *COW/LTMR* OX4 .. 62 C2 ▉
Jackdaw La *COW/LTMR* OX4 .... 50 D1
Jackies La *WHLY* OX33 .... 54 D1
Jackman Cl *ABGD* OX14 .... 73 H2
Jackson Dr *OX/KTN* OX1 .... 60 C1
Jackson Rd *OXN/BOT/CM* OX2 .... 32 A2
Jack Straw's La *HEAD* OX3 .... 41 F2
James St *COW/LTMR* OX4 .... 41 E5
James Wolfe Rd *COW/LTMR* OX4 .. 52 B1
Janaway Pl *COW/LTMR* OX4 .... 61 F2
Jarn Wy *OXN/BOT/CM* OX2 .... 59 E2
Jasmine Cl *COW/LTMR* OX4 .... 62 C1 ▉
Jericho St *OXN/BOT/CM* OX2 .... 2 A3
Jerome Wy *KID* OX5 .... 6 C3
Jersey Rd *COW/LTMR* OX4 .... 51 F5
Jeune St *COW/LTMR* OX4 .... 3 J6
Joan Lawrence Pl *HEAD* OX3 .. 42 B4 ▉
John Buchan Rd *HEAD* OX3 .... 33 G5
John Garne Wy *HEAD* OX3 .... 3 K3
John Lopes Rd *WIT/EY* OX8 .... 28 B3 ▉
John Mason Rd *ABGD* OX14 .... 73 H1
John Morris Rd *ABGD* OX14 .... 73 F4
John Snow Pl *HEAD* OX3 .... 42 B2
John Towle Cl *OX/KTN* OX1 .... 50 C3
Jordan Hl *OXN/BOT/CM* OX2 .... 21 H5
Jourdain Rd *COW/LTMR* OX4 .... 52 C5
Jowett Wk *OX/KTN* OX1 .... 3 F4
Judges Cl *KID* OX5 .... 13 E4
Junction Rd *COW/LTMR* OX4 .... 52 A2
Juniper Dr *COW/LTMR* OX4 .... 62 C1
Juxon St *OXN/BOT/CM* OX2 .... 2 A2
 OXN/BOT/CM OX2 .... 39 H2

K

Kames Cl *COW/LTMR* OX4 .... 51 G3
Keble Rd *OX/KTN* OX1 .... 2 C3
Keene Cl *COW/LTMR* OX4 .... 61 G3
Kelburne Rd *COW/LTMR* OX4 .... 51 G4
Kelham Hall Dr *WHLY* OX33 .... 54 C1
Kelly's Rd *WHLY* OX33 .... 53 H1
Kempson Crs *COW/LTMR* OX4 .... 61 F1
Kempster Cl *ABGD* OX14 .... 74 A1 ▉
Kendall Crs *OXN/BOT/CM* OX2 .... 32 A1
Kenilworth Av *COW/LTMR* OX4 .. 51 G1
Kenilworth Rd
 OXN/BOT/CM OX2 .... 47 H4 ▉
Kennedy Cl *HEAD* OX3 .... 52 B1
Kennet Cl *WGFD* OX10 .... 77 F5
Kennet Rd *ABGD* OX14 .... 68 A5
Kennett Rd *HEAD* OX3 .... 41 H2
Kennington Rd *ABGD* OX14 .... 68 D3
 OX/KTN OX1 .... 60 D1
Kensington Cl *ABGD* OX14 .... 74 A1 ▉
Kent Cl *ABGD* OX14 .... 74 A1 ▉
 COW/LTMR OX4 .... 52 B5
Kenville Rd *OX/KTN* OX1 .... 60 C1
Kersington Crs *COW/LTMR* OX4 .. 52 A5
Kerwood Cl *WDSTK* OX20 .... 5 E2
Kestrel Crs *COW/LTMR* OX4 .... 62 A1
Kestrel Pl *COW/LTMR* OX4 .... 62 A1 ▉
Kestrel Rd *MCHM/KBPZ* OX13 .... 66 C4
Keydale Rd *WHLY* OX33 .... 44 A5
Kidlington Rd *KID* OX5 .... 14 D3
Kiln Cl *COW/LTMR* OX4 .... 61 G3
Kiln La *HEAD* OX3 .... 42 C3
 STAD OX44 .... 63 F2
 WHLY OX33 .... 44 B5
Kimber Cl *WHLY* OX33 .... 44 B5
Kimber Rd *ABGD* OX14 .... 72 C2
Kineton Rd *OXN/BOT/CM* OX2 .... 39 H4
King Edward St *OX/KTN* OX1 .... 2 E6 ▉
Kingfisher Cl *ABGD* OX14 .... 73 G5
Kingfisher Gn *COW/LTMR* OX4 .. 62 C2
King's Cross Rd
 OXN/BOT/CM OX2 .... 32 A3
King's Head La *KID* OX5 .... 15 E3
King's Mill La *HEAD* OX3 .... 3 J4
Kingston Cl *ABGD* OX14 .... 73 G1 ▉
Kingston Hts *WIT/EY* OX8 .... 8 A5 ▉
Kingston Rd *OXN/BOT/CM* OX2 .... 40 A1
King St *OXN/BOT/CM* OX2 .... 2 A2
Kings Way Dr *KID* OX5 .... 13 H4
Kirby Pl *COW/LTMR* OX4 .... 52 A3 ▉
Kirk Cl *OX/KTN* OX1 .... 60 D3
 OXN/BOT/CM OX2 .... 31 H1
Knapp Cl *ABGD* OX14 .... 73 E1
Knights Rd *COW/LTMR* OX4 .... 62 A1
Knolles Rd *COW/LTMR* OX4 .... 51 H3

Knollys Cl *ABGD* OX14 ....
Kybald St *OX/KTN* OX1 ....
Kysbie Cl *ABGD* OX14 ....

L

Laburnam Av *MCHM/KBPZ* OX13
Laburnum Av *MCHM/KBPZ* OX13
Laburnum Crs *KID* OX5 ....
Laburnum Rd *OXN/BOT/CM* OX2
Ladder Hl *WHLY* OX33 ....
Ladenham Rd *COW/LTMR* OX4 ..
Ladygrove Paddock
 ABGD OX14 ....
Ladywell Cl *WIT/EY* OX8 ....
Lakefield Rd *COW/LTMR* OX4 ....
Lakeside Rd *OXN/BOT/CM* OX2 ..
Lakesmere Cl *KID* OX5 ....
Lake St *OX/KTN* OX1 ....
Lamarsh Rd *OXN/BOT/CM* OX2 ..
Lamb La *WDSTK* OX20 ....
Lamborough Hl
 MCHM/KBPZ OX13 ....
Lambourn Rd *COW/LTMR* OX4 ....
Lambrick Wy *ABGD* OX14 ....
Lambs Cl *KID* OX5 ....
Lambton Cl *COW/LTMR* OX4 ....
Lammas Cl *ABGD* OX14 ....
Lane Cl *KID* OX5 ....
The Lane *STAD* OX44 ....
Langford La *KID* OX5 ....
Langley Cl *HEAD* OX3 ....
Langley Rd *ABGD* OX14 ....
Lanham Wy *COW/LTMR* OX4 ....
Lansdowne Rd
 MCHM/KBPZ OX13 ....
Larch End *STAD* OX44 ....
The Larches *HEAD* OX3 ....
Larkfields *HEAD* OX3 ....
Larkhill Pl *ABGD* OX14 ....
Larkhill Rd *ABGD* OX14 ....
Larkins La *HEAD* OX3 ....
Lashford La *MCHM/KBPZ* OX13 ...
Lathbury Rd *OXN/BOT/CM* OX2 ..
Latimer Rd *HEAD* OX3 ....
Laurel Farm Cl *HEAD* OX3 ....
Lawrence Rd *COW/LTMR* OX4 ....
Lay Av *WGFD* OX10 ....
Leach Rd *WGFD* OX10 ....
Leafield Rd *OXN/BOT/CM* OX2 ....
Leckford Pl *OXN/BOT/CM* OX2 ....
Leckford Rd *OXN/BOT/CM* OX2 ....
Ledgers Cl *COW/LTMR* OX4 ....
Lee Av *ABGD* OX14 ....
Lee Cl *KID* OX5 ....
Leiden Rd *HEAD* OX3 ....
Leigh Cl *WIT/EY* OX8 ....
Leigh Cft *MCHM/KBPZ* OX13 ....
Lenthal Rd *KID* OX5 ....
Lenthall Rd *ABGD* OX14 ....
 COW/LTMR OX4 ....
Leon Cl *COW/LTMR* OX4 ....
Leopold St *COW/LTMR* OX4 ....
Letcombe Av *ABGD* OX14 ....
Levery Cl *ABGD* OX14 ....
Lewell Av *HEAD* OX3 ....
Lewin Cl *COW/LTMR* OX4 ....
Lewis Cl *HEAD* OX3 ....
Leyshon Rd *WHLY* OX33 ....
Leys Pl *COW/LTMR* OX4 ....
Leys Rd *OXN/BOT/CM* OX2 ....
The Ley *WDSTK* OX20 ....
Liddell Rd *COW/LTMR* OX4 ....
Liddiard Cl *OX/KTN* OX1 ....
Lime Rd *OXN/BOT/CM* OX2 ....
Lime Wk *HEAD* OX3 ....
Lincoln Rd *OX/KTN* OX1 ....
Lincombe La *OX/KTN* OX1 ....
Lincraft Cl *KID* OX5 ....
Lindsay Dr *ABGD* OX14 ....
Linkside Rd *OXN/BOT/CM* OX2 ....
Links Rd *OX/KTN* OX1 ....
The Link *HEAD* OX3 ....
 HEAD OX3 ....
Linnet Cl *COW/LTMR* OX4 ....
Linton Rd *OXN/BOT/CM* OX2 ....
Little Acreage *HEAD* OX3 ....
Little Blenheim *KID* OX5 ....
Little Brewery St
 COW/LTMR OX4 ....
Little Bury *COW/LTMR* OX4 ....
Little Clarendon St *OX/KTN* OX1 ...
Littlegate *OX/KTN* OX1 ....
Littlehay Rd *COW/LTMR* OX4 ....
Little Howe Cl *ABGD* OX14 ....
Littlemore Rd *COW/LTMR* OX4 ....

orth Rd *WHLY* OX33 .... 44 A5
Rd *COW/LTMR* OX4 .... 62 C1
s *KID* OX5 .... 21 F1
rt Crs *COW/LTMR* OX4 .... 52 A4
ay *ABGD* OX14 .... 78 B3
Av *WGFD* OX10 .... 77 F4
CI *HEAD* OX3 .... 33 E3
Rd *WDSTK* OX20 .... 10 C3
Rd *OX/KTN* OX1.. .... 3 F6
rd St *ABGD* OX14 .... 73 G2
Rd *HEAD* OX3 .... 41 H2
OX33 .... 44 D5
HEAD OX3 .... 42 B5
BOT/CM OX2.. .... 38 C5
llow Dr *ABGD* OX14 .... 72 D4
ord CI *OX/KTN* OX1 .... 50 B1
urlong Rd
M/KBPZ OX13 .... 67 E2
and *COW/LTMR* OX4 .... 62 B2
ands Rd *COW/LTMR* OX4 .. 52 B5
ead *ABGD* OX14 .... 67 F5
ow *MCHM/KBPZ* OX13.. .... 67 E4
Av *COW/LTMR* OX4 .... 51 G5
all St *OX/KTN* OX1.. .... 3 F5
orth Rd *OXN/BOT/CM* OX2.. 39 H2
le Rd *OXN/BOT/CM* OX2.. 32 A3
ce CI *ABGD* OX14 .... 67 H3
ce Dr *KID* OX5 .... 13 H4
Whitley Rd
BOT/CM OX2.. .... 37 F5
ll *ABGD* OX14 .... 67 H3
Dr *ABGD* OX14 .... 73 E5
e Rd *OXN/BOT/CM* OX2.. 32 B2
rd Rd *ABGD* OX14 .... 68 A4
Ct *OX/KTN* OX1 .... 40 B5
l *HEAD* OX3 .... 42 C1
HEAD OX3 .... 52 A1
l *ABGD* OX14 .... 78 C2
Wy *ABGD* OX14 .... 68 A4
ook CI *WIT/EY* OX8 .... 26 B5
orth CI *HEAD* OX3 .... 42 B1
d *KID* OX5 .... 12 D3
CI *ABGD* OX14 .... 68 A4
l *HEAD* OX3 .... 41 E1
La *WIT/EY* OX8 .... 19 G5
Rd *COW/LTMR* OX4 .... 51 F3

M

ey CI *ABGD* OX14 .... 72 D4
len Br *OX/KTN* OX1 .... 3 G6
len Rd *COW/LTMR* OX4 .... 51 E1
len St *OX/KTN* OX1 .... 2 C5
tte St *ABGD* OX14 .... 73 G2
lia CI *KID* OX5 .... 13 F5
e La *OX/KTN* OX1 .... 2 E6
oft Rd *COW/LTMR* OX4 .... 51 H3
v *COW/LTMR* OX4 .... 61 H3
l *ABGD* OX14 .... 81 E5
EY OX8 .... 9 G3
d Rd *HEAD* OX3 .... 42 C1
l CI *COW/LTMR* OX4 .... 62 A1
ld *HEAD* OX3 .... 33 F5
ville CI *ABGD* OX14 .... 67 H4
l *ABGD* OX14 .... 78 C3
e OX8 .... 19 F5
Ct *ABGD* OX14 .... 73 F3
Dr *WHLY* OX33 .... 53 F2
Farm Rd *WHLY* OX33 .... 53 F2
Gv *OX/KTN* OX1 .... 60 D4
PI *OX/KTN* OX1.. .... 3 G4
Rd *MCHM/KBPZ* OX13.. .... 58 B4
TN OX1.. .... 3 G4
TN OX1 .... 50 A3
TK OX20 .... 4 D2
TK OX20 .... 11 E3
Wy *KID* OX5 .... 13 F2
l *WIT/EY* OX8 .... 17 H1
eld Rd *OX/KTN* OX1.. .... 2 E3
Wy *COW/LTMR* OX4 .. 41 F5
Av *KID* OX5 .... 13 F5
l *OXN/BOT/CM* OX2.. 39 E5
am Rd *ABGD* OX14 .... 78 B3
ret Rd *HEAD* OX3 .... 42 A3
ld CI *COW/LTMR* OX4 .. 62 C2
am CI *COW/LTMR* OX4 .. 62 D1
: PI *WDSTK* OX20.. .... 4 D3
st St *OX/KTN* OX1.. .... 3 G4
d *HEAD* OX3 .... 42 B3

Marlborough Av *KID* OX5 .... 13 E2
Marlborough CI
 COW/LTMR OX4 .... 61 G1
 WIT/EY OX8 .... 28 B2
Marlborough Ct
 OXN/BOT/CM OX2 .... 39 G4
Marlborough Crs *WDSTK* OX20 ... 4 D2
 WIT/EY OX8 .... 9 F4
Marlborough Dr *WIT/EY* OX8... 29 F1
Marlborough PI *WIT/EY* OX8 .... 28 B2
Marlborough Rd *OX/KTN* OX1 .... 50 B1
Marriott CI *COW/LTMR* OX4 .... 32 A1
Marshall Rd *COW/LTMR* OX4 .... 52 A2
Marsh CI *KID* OX5 .... 20 D2
Marsh St *ABGD* OX14 .... 73 G1
Marsh La *HEAD* OX3 .... 33 F5
Marsh Rd *COW/LTMR* OX4 .... 51 H2
Marston St *COW/LTMR* OX4 .... 41 E5
Marylands Gn *STAD* OX44 .... 71 G4
Mascall Av *HEAD* OX3 .... 52 B1
Masefield Crs *ABGD* OX14.. .... 72 D4
Masey CI *HEAD* OX3 .... 42 A4
Masons Rd *HEAD* OX3 .... 42 B4
Mather Rd *HEAD* OX3 .... 42 B4
Mathews Wy
 MCHM/KBPZ OX13 .... 58 C5
Mattock CI *HEAD* OX3 .... 42 A3
Mattock Wy *ABGD* OX14 .... 68 A3
Mavor CI *WDSTK* OX20 .... 4 D2
Mayfair Rd *COW/LTMR* OX4 .... 51 G4
Mayfield Rd *OXN/BOT/CM* OX2 .... 32 A3
 OXN/BOT/CM OX2.. .... 37 E3
Mayott's Rd *ABGD* OX14 .... 73 F2
Meaden Hl *HEAD* OX3 .... 33 G5
Meadow CI *WIT/EY* OX8 .... 37 E2
Meadow La *COW/LTMR* OX4 .... 50 D1
Meadow Prospect
 OXN/BOT/CM OX2 .... 31 E2
Meadowside *ABGD* OX14 .... 73 F3
Meadow Vw *KID* OX5 .... 13 F2
Meadow View Rd *OX/KTN* OX1 ... 60 D3
Meadow Wk *WDSTK* OX20 .... 5 F3
Meadow Wy *KID* OX5 .... 20 C2
Meads CI *ABGD* OX14 .... 78 C2
Mead Wy *KID* OX5 .... 13 F2
Medlicott Dr *ABGD* OX14 .... 72 D3
Medway CI *MCHM/KBPZ* OX13 .... 66 D3
Medway Rd *MCHM/KBPZ* OX13.. ... 66 D3
Melbourne CI
 COW/LTMR OX4 .... 62 C2
Mercury Rd *COW/LTMR* OX4 .... 62 D1
Mere Rd *OXN/BOT/CM* OX2 .... 31 G2
Merewood Av *HEAD* OX3 .... 42 D1
Merlin Rd *COW/LTMR* OX4 .... 62 B1
 MCHM/KBPZ OX13 .... 66 C4
Merrivale Sq
 OXN/BOT/CM OX2 .... 39 H1
Merton CI *ABGD* OX14 .... 28 A3
Merton Gv *OX/KTN* OX1 .... 2 E6
Merton St *OX/KTN* OX1 .... 3 F6
Merton Wy *KID* OX5.. .... 20 C2
Metcalf CI *ABGD* OX14 .... 73 F5
Meyseys Rd *HEAD* OX3 .... 52 C1
Mickle Wy *WHLY* OX33 .... 43 H1
Middle Rd *WHLY* OX33 .... 35 G3
Middle St *KID* OX5 .... 15 E3
Middle Wy *KID* OX5 .... 15 E3
 OXN/BOT/CM OX2 .... 31 H3
Midget CI *ABGD* OX14 .... 73 G2
Mileway Gdns *HEAD* OX3 .... 41 H4
Millbank *OXN/BOT/CM* OX2.. .... 39 H5
Mill End *KID* OX5 .... 13 H3
Miller Rd *WHLY* OX33 .... 54 D1
Miller's Acre
 OXN/BOT/CM OX2 .... 32 A1
Mill La *ABGD* OX14 .... 79 G5
 COW/LTMR OX4 .... 51 E4
 HEAD OX3 .... 32 D3
 WIT/EY OX8 .... 28 C1
Millmoor Crs *WIT/EY* OX8 .... 28 B2
Mill Paddock *ABGD* OX14 .... 73 G3
Mill Rd *ABGD* OX14 .... 72 D4
 OXN/BOT/CM OX2 .... 31 E2
Mill St *KID* OX5 .... 13 H3
 OXN/BOT/CM OX2 .... 39 H4
 WHLY OX33 .... 35 G3
 WIT/EY OX8 .... 28 B3
Millway La *MCHM/KBPZ* OX13.. ... 56 B5
Millwood End *WIT/EY* OX8 .... 9 F2
Millwood V *WIT/EY* OX8 .... 9 F3
Milne PI *HEAD* OX3 .... 41 G1
Milton Crs *WHLY* OX33 .... 44 A1
Milton Rd *COW/LTMR* OX4 .... 51 G2

Minchery Rd *COW/LTMR* OX4 .... 61 G1
Minchins CI *ABGD* OX14.. .... 74 B1
Minster Rd *COW/LTMR* OX4 .... 41 F5
Mistletoe Gn *COW/LTMR* OX4 .... 62 B2
Mitchell CI *MCHM/KBPZ* OX13 .... 58 B5
Moberly CI *COW/LTMR* OX4 .... 41 E5
Mole PI *COW/LTMR* OX4 .... 62 C2
Monks CI *COW/LTMR* OX4 .... 62 A1
Monmouth Rd *OX/KTN* OX1.. .... 50 C3
Mons Wy *ABGD* OX14 .... 67 E5
Montagu Rd *OXN/BOT/CM* OX2.. 38 B5
Moody Rd *HEAD* OX3 .... 3 K2
Moorbank *COW/LTMR* OX4 .... 52 B5
The Moorlands *KID* OX5 .... 13 E2
The Moors *KID* OX5 .... 13 E2
Moreton Rd *OXN/BOT/CM* OX2 .... 32 A4
Morland CI *WHLY* OX33 .... 44 C5
Morrell Av *COW/LTMR* OX4 .... 3 K6
Morrell CI *KID* OX5 .... 13 E4
Morrell Crs *COW/LTMR* OX4 .... 61 F1
Morris Crs *COW/LTMR* OX4 .... 51 G2
Mortimer Dr *HEAD* OX3 .... 40 D1
Mortimer Rd *COW/LTMR* OX4 .... 51 E5
Morton Av *KID* OX5 .... 13 F5
Morton CI *ABGD* OX14 .... 74 B1
 KID OX5 .... 13 F4
The Motte *ABGD* OX14 .... 73 G1
Mount PI *OXN/BOT/CM* OX2 .... 39 H3
Mount St *OXN/BOT/CM* OX2 .... 39 H3
Mulberry Dr *WHLY* OX33 .... 44 C5
Mulcaster Av *KID* OX5 .... 13 G4
Mullard Wy *ABGD* OX14 .... 73 F2
Museum Rd *OX/KTN* OX1 .... 2 D5
Musson CI *ABGD* OX14 .... 73 F3
Myrtle CI *WIT/EY* OX8 .... 9 G3

N

Napier Rd *COW/LTMR* OX4 .... 52 A4
Nash Dr *ABGD* OX14 .... 72 D3
Nash La *WIT/EY* OX8 .... 9 F4
Nelson St *OXN/BOT/CM* OX2 .... 2 A4
Nene Rd *MCHM/KBPZ* OX13 .... 66 D4
Netherton Rd *MCHM/KBPZ* OX13.. 56 C5
Netherwoods Rd *HEAD* OX3 .... 42 C3
Nettlebed Md *COW/LTMR* OX4 .. 62 B2
New College La *OX/KTN* OX1 .... 2 E5
New Cross Rd *HEAD* OX3 .... 42 B2
New High St *HEAD* OX3 .... 41 H3
New Inn Hall St *OX/KTN* OX1 .... 2 C6
New Inn Rd *OXN/BOT/CM* OX2 .... 24 D5
Newland CI *WIT/EY* OX8 .... 28 B3
Newland St *WIT/EY* OX8 .... 28 B2
Newlin CI *COW/LTMR* OX4 .... 51 H5
Newman La *ABGD* OX14 .... 78 C2
Newman Rd *COW/LTMR* OX4 .... 51 G5
Newport CI *KID* OX5 .... 13 E5
New Rd *ABGD* OX14 .... 68 D3
 OX/KTN OX1.. .... 2 B6
 WDSTK OX20 .... 5 E3
 WIT/EY OX8 .... 9 G3
New St *ABGD* OX14 .... 73 G2
Newton Rd *OX/KTN* OX1 .... 50 B1
Nicholas Av *HEAD* OX3 .... 41 E1
Nicholson Rd *HEAD* OX3 .... 3 J1
Nightingale Av *COW/LTMR* OX4.. 62 C2
Ninth Av *HEAD* OX3 .... 52 C1
Nixon Rd *COW/LTMR* OX4 .... 51 E3
Nobles CI *ABGD* OX14 .... 38 B5
Nobles La *OXN/BOT/CM* OX2 .... 38 B5
Norbrook CI *ABGD* OX14 .... 68 B4
Norfolk CI *ABGD* OX14 .... 68 C4
Norfolk St *OX/KTN* OX1.. .... 2 C7
Norham Gdns *OXN/BOT/CM* OX2 ... 2 C1
Norham Rd *OXN/BOT/CM* OX2 .... 40 B1
Norman Av *ABGD* OX14.. .... 67 H5
Normandy CI *COW/LTMR* OX4 .... 52 B3
Norman Smith Rd
 COW/LTMR OX4 .... 62 C2
Norreys Av *OX/KTN* OX1 .... 50 C2
Norreys Rd *OXN/BOT/CM* OX2 .... 48 A3
Norris CI *ABGD* OX14 .... 68 A4
Northampton Rd *OX/KTN* OX1 .... 50 C3
North Av *ABGD* OX14 .... 67 H4
Northcourt La *ABGD* OX14 .... 67 H5
Northcourt Rd *ABGD* OX14 .... 67 H5
Northcourt Wk *ABGD* OX14 .... 73 H1
Northern By-pass Rd *HEAD* OX3.. 33 G5
Northern by Pass Rd
 OXN/BOT/CM OX2 .... 21 E5
Northern By-pass Rd
 OXN/BOT/CM OX2 .... 32 C2
Northfield Rd *ABGD* OX14 .... 67 H3
 HEAD OX3 .... 42 B1
North Hinksey La
 OXN/BOT/CM OX2.. .... 39 F5

Northmoor Rd
 OXN/BOT/CM OX2.. .... 32 B5
North Parade Av
 OXN/BOT/CM OX2.. .... 40 A1
North PI *HEAD* OX3 .... 42 A2
North Quay *ABGD* OX14 .... 73 G5
North St *KID* OX5 .... 15 E3
North Wy *HEAD* OX3 .... 42 B1
 OXN/BOT/CM OX2 .... 31 H1
Norton CI *HEAD* OX3 .... 42 A3
Nowell Rd *COW/LTMR* OX4 .... 51 F5
Nuffield Rd *HEAD* OX3.. .... 42 B5
Nuffield Wy *ABGD* OX14 .... 72 D2
Nuneham Sq *ABGD* OX14 .... 73 F1
Nurseries Rd *KID* OX5 .... 13 E4
Nursery CI *HEAD* OX3 .... 41 H3
Nursery Rd *WIT/EY* OX8 .... 8 B5
The Nursery *ABGD* OX14 .... 79 H4
Nuthatch CI *COW/LTMR* OX4 .... 62 B2
Nyatt Rd *ABGD* OX14 .... 74 B1
Nye Bevan CI *COW/LTMR* OX4 .... 41 F5

O

Oak Av *ABGD* OX14.. .... 60 D5
Oak Dr *KID* OX5 .... 13 G4
Oakes La *OXN/BOT/CM* OX2.. .... 37 F3
Oakesmere *MCHM/KBPZ* OX13 .... 57 E5
Oakland CI *WIT/EY* OX8.. .... 9 E5
Oak Mill CI *ABGD* OX14 .... 73 E3
Oakthorpe PI
 OXN/BOT/CM OX2.. .... 32 A4
Oakthorpe Rd *OXN/BOT/CM* OX2.. 32 A4
Oatlands Rd *OXN/BOT/CM* OX2 ... 39 G4
Observatory St *OXN/BOT/CM* OX2 .. 2 B2
Ock Dr *WGFD* OX10 .... 77 G4
Ock St *ABGD* OX14 .... 73 F3
Old Chapel CI *KID* OX5 .... 13 F3
Old Farm CI *ABGD* OX14 .... 74 B1
Old Fld *STAD* OX44 .... 65 H4
Old Greyfriars St *OX/KTN* OX1 .... 2 C7
Old High St *HEAD* OX3 .... 42 A1
Old London Rd *WHLY* OX33 .... 44 D5
Old Marston Rd *HEAD* OX3 .... 41 E1
Old Nursery Vw *OX/KTN* OX1 .... 50 C5
The Old Pound
 MCHM/KBPZ OX13 .... 66 C1
Old Rd *HEAD* OX3 .... 42 A4
 WHLY OX33 .... 43 G5
Old Witney Rd *WIT/EY* OX8 .... 27 H2
Oliver Rd *COW/LTMR* OX4 .... 52 B3
Orchard CI *WHLY* OX33 .... 54 C1
 WIT/EY OX8 .... 19 F5
Orchard Field La *WDSTK* OX20.. ... 5 G5
Orchard La *OX/KTN* OX1 .... 58 D2
Orchard Rd *OXN/BOT/CM* OX2 .... 38 B5
The Orchard *WIT/EY* OX8 .... 28 C5
Orchard Wy *COW/LTMR* OX4 .... 51 H5
 KID OX5 .... 13 G4
Oriel St *OX/KTN* OX1 .... 2 E6
Orpwood Wy *ABGD* OX14 .... 72 D3
Osberton Rd *OXN/BOT/CM* OX2 ... 31 H3
Osborne CI *KID* OX5 .... 13 E5
 OXN/BOT/CM OX2 .... 31 G2
Osler Rd *HEAD* OX3 .... 41 H2
Osney La *OX/KTN* OX1 .... 2 A6
Osney Md *OXN/BOT/CM* OX2.. .... 39 H4
Osney Md *OXN/BOT/CM* OX2 .... 39 H5
Oswestry Rd *OX/KTN* OX1 .... 50 C3
Otmoor La *HEAD* OX3 .... 25 E3
Otters Reach *OX/KTN* OX1 .... 60 D2
Otwell CI *ABGD* OX14 .... 68 A4
Ouseley CI *HEAD* OX3 .... 41 E1
Outram Rd *COW/LTMR* OX4 .... 51 G3
The Oval *COW/LTMR* OX4 .... 51 G3
Overbrooke Gdns
 COW/LTMR OX4 .... 62 D1
Overdale CI *HEAD* OX3 .... 42 B1
Owlington CI *OXN/BOT/CM* OX2 ... 38 D4
Oxeye Ct *COW/LTMR* OX4 .... 62 B3
Oxford Canal Wk *KID* OX5 .... 21 E4
 OXN/BOT/CM OX2 .... 31 H5
Oxford Rd *ABGD* OX14 .... 67 H4
 ABGD OX14 .... 73 G1
 ABGD OX14 .... 76 B3
 COW/LTMR OX4.. .... 51 G2
 COW/LTMR OX4 .... 51 G5
 COW/LTMR OX4 .... 52 C3
 COW/LTMR OX4 .... 61 G1
 HEAD OX3 .... 33 E4
 KID OX5 .... 7 H2
 KID OX5 .... 13 F4
 KID OX5 .... 14 A2
 KID OX5 .... 21 H3
 OXN/BOT/CM OX2.. .... 48 A3
 STAD OX44 .... 53 E3

WDSTK OX20 .... 5 F4
WIT/EY OX8 .... 28 C3
Oxfordshire Circular Wks
WIT/EY OX8 .... 28 C5
Oxford St WDSTK OX20 .... 4 D3
Oxpens Rd OX/KTN OX1 .... 2 A6

P

The Paddocks KID OX5 .... 20 C2 🔟
The Paddock OXN/BOT/CM OX4 .... 60 D4
Paddox Cl OXN/BOT/CM OX2 ...... 31 H2
Paget Rd COW/LTMR OX4 .... 52 B2
Pagisters'Rd ABGD OX14 .... 68 B4
Palmer Rd HEAD OX3 .... 42 B4
Paradise Sq OX/KTN OX1 .... 2 B7
Paradise St OX/KTN OX1 .... 2 B6 🔟
Park Av KID OX5 .... 13 E2
Park Cl KID OX5 .... 20 C3
    OXN/BOT/CM OX2 .... 22 A5
    WDSTK OX20 .... 11 E1
    WIT/EY OX8 .... 16 B1
Park Crs ABGD OX14 .... 73 E2
Park End Pl OX/KTN OX1 .... 2 B6 🔟
Park End St OX/KTN OX1 .... 2 A5
Parker St COW/LTMR OX4 .... 51 E2
Park HI WHLY OX33 .... 44 B4
Parklands WIT/EY OX8 .... 9 E5
Park La MCHM/KBPZ OX13 .... 56 D4
    WDSTK OX20 .... 4 D3
    WDSTK OX20 .... 11 E1
    WIT/EY OX8 .... 10 A2
Park Rd ABGD OX14 .... 73 E2
    WIT/EY OX8 .... 16 A1
Park Side WDSTK OX20 .... 5 F3
Parkside WIT/EY OX8 .... 16 B1
Parks Rd OX/KTN OX1 .... 2 D4
Park St WDSTK OX20 .... 4 D3
    WDSTK OX20 .... 11 E2
The Park OXN/BOT/CM OX2 .... 47 H3
Park Town OXN/BOT/CM OX2 ..... 40 B1
Park Wy HEAD OX3 .... 33 E3
Parry Cl HEAD OX3 .... 3 J1
Parsons Md ABGD OX14 .... 67 F5
Parsons Pl COW/LTMR OX4 .... 41 F5
Partridge Pl KID OX5 .... 12 D3
Partridge Wk COW/LTMR OX4 .... 62 D2 🔟
Pattison Pl COW/LTMR OX4 ...... 51 F5 🔟
Pauling Rd HEAD OX3 .... 42 B4
Peachcroft Rd ABGD OX14........ 68 B4
Peacock Rd HEAD OX3 .... 3 K2
Peartree Cl COW/LTMR OX4 .... 62 C2 🔟🔟
Peat Moors HEAD OX3 .... 42 A5
Peel Pl OX/KTN OX1 .... 50 C3
Peep-o-day La ABGD OX14......... 79 F2
Pegasus Rd COW/LTMR OX4 ...... 62 B2
Pelican Pl WIT/EY OX8 .... 28 B2
Pembroke Sq OX/KTN OX1 ...... 2 D7 🔟
Pembroke St OX/KTN OX1 .... 2 D6
Pen La ABGD OX14 .... 67 G1
    MCHM/KBPZ OX13 .... 67 G1
Penn Cl ABGD OX14 .... 68 B4 🔟
Pennycress Rd
    COW/LTMR OX4 .... 62 D1 🔟
Pennywell Dr OXN/BOT/CM OX2.... 22 A5
Penson's Gdns COW/LTMR OX4 .. 3 H6 🔟
Peppercorn Av HEAD OX3 ...... 42 B5 🔟
Percy St COW/LTMR OX4 .... 51 E2
Peregrine Pl COW/LTMR OX4 ..... 62 C1
Periwinkle Pl COW/LTMR OX4 .... 62 C1
Perkins OX/KTN OX1 .... 60 C1
Perrin St HEAD OX3 .... 41 H3
Peterley Rd COW/LTMR OX4 ...... 52 C2
Peter's Wy COW/LTMR OX4 .... 61 H1
Pether Rd HEAD OX3.............. 42 B4
Petre Pl KID OX5 .... 13 G3
Pettiwell STAD OX44 .... 63 G3
Pheasant Wk COW/LTMR OX4 .... 61 F2
The Phelps KID OX5.............. 13 E4
Phipps Rd COW/LTMR OX4 .... 52 B1
Picklers Hl ABGD OX14 .... 67 H4
Pickett Av HEAD OX3............. 52 B1
Pigeon House La WIT/EY OX8 ..... 17 C1
Pike Ter OX/KTN OX1 .... 2 C7
Pimpernel Cl COW/LTMR OX4 .... 62 D1 🔟
Pine Cl COW/LTMR OX4 .... 52 D5 🔟
Pinkhill La WIT/EY OX8 .... 28 B4
Pinnocks Wy OXN/BOT/CM OX2 .. 38 C5
Pinsley Rd WIT/EY OX8 .... 9 G4
Piper St HEAD OX3 .... 42 A3
Pipit Cl COW/LTMR OX4 .... 62 B2 🔟🔟
Pipkin Wy COW/LTMR OX4 ...... 51 F2 🔟
Pitts Rd HEAD OX3 .... 42 B2
Pixey Pl OXN/BOT/CM OX2 .... 31 G2 🔟
The Plain OX/KTN OX1............. 3 G6
Plane Tree Wy WDSTK OX20....... 5 F3

Plantation Rd OXN/BOT/CM OX2 .... 2 A1
Plater Dr OXN/BOT/CM OX2....... 39 H1
Playfield Rd OX/KTN OX1 .... 60 D4
Ploughley Cl KID OX5 .... 13 E4 🔟
Pochard Pl COW/LTMR OX4 .... 62 C2 🔟🔟
Polecat End La WHLY OX33 ...... 44 A1
Polstead Rd OXN/BOT/CM OX2 ... 40 A1
Pond Cl HEAD OX3 .... 42 D2
Ponds La HEAD OX3................ 33 E4
Pony Rd COW/LTMR OX4 .... 52 C2
Poplar Cl KID OX5 .... 13 G5 🔟
    STAD OX44 .... 63 F1
Poplar Gv OX/KTN OX1 .... 60 D3
Poplar Rd COW/LTMR OX4 .... 38 D4
Portland Rd OXN/BOT/CM OX2 ... 32 A3
Potenger Wy ABGD OX14 .... 73 E3
Pottery Piece COW/LTMR OX4 ... 62 B2
Pottle Cl OXN/BOT/CM OX2 ...... 38 C4
Poulton Pl COW/LTMR OX4 ...... 52 C5
Pound Cl KID OX5................ 20 C2
Pound Field Cl HEAD OX3 ...... 34 B5
Pound La WHLY OX33 .... 35 F3
    WIT/EY OX8 .... 19 F5
Powell Wk WHLY OX33 .... 44 A1
Preachers La OX/KTN OX1 .... 2 C7
    OX/KTN OX1 .... 40 B5 🔟🔟
Preston Rd ABGD OX14........... 73 E4
Prestwich Pl OXN/BOT/CM OX2 .. 39 G4
Prichard Rd HEAD OX3 .... 41 F2
Primrose Pl COW/LTMR OX4 .... 62 C2 🔟🔟
Prince Gv ABGD OX14 .... 67 H3
Princes Ride WDSTK OX20 .... 5 F3
Princes St COW/LTMR OX4 .... 3 K7
Prior's Forge OXN/BOT/CM OX2 .. 32 A1
Priory Rd COW/LTMR OX4 .... 52 C5
Pritchard Cl WGFD OX10 .... 77 F3 🔟
Pudsey Cl ABGD OX14 .... 73 E3
Pulker Cl COW/LTMR OX4 ...... 51 H4 🔟
Pullens Fld HEAD OX3............. 41 F3
Pullens La HEAD OX3 .... 41 F3
Purcell Rd HEAD OX3 .... 3 J1
Purslane ABGD OX14 .... 74 A1
Pusey La OX/KTN OX1 .... 2 C4
Pusey Pl OX/KTN OX1 .... 2 C4 🔟
Pusey St OX/KTN OX1 .... 2 C4
Pykes Cl ABGD OX14 .... 68 A4
Pytenry Cl ABGD OX14 .... 68 A3

Q

The Quadrant ABGD OX14 .... 74 A2
Quarry End KID OX5 .... 12 C4
Quarry High St HEAD OX3 .... 42 B2
Quarry Hollow HEAD OX3 .... 42 B3
Quarry Rd HEAD OX3 .... 42 B3
    MCHM/KBPZ OX13 .... 59 H4
Quarry School Pl HEAD OX3 ..... 42 B3 🔟
Quartermain Cl
    COW/LTMR OX4 .... 51 F2 🔟
Queens Av KID OX5 .... 13 H4
Queens Cl OXN/BOT/CM OX2 .... 38 C5
    WIT/EY OX8 .... 28 B5
Queen's La OX/KTN OX1 .... 2 E5 🔟
    WIT/EY OX8 .... 28 B3
Queen St ABGD OX14 .... 73 G2 🔟
    OX/KTN OX1 .... 2 C6
    WIT/EY OX8 .... 28 B3

R

Radcliffe Rd COW/LTMR OX4 ...... 51 E3
Radcliffe Sq OX/KTN OX1 .... 2 E5 🔟
Radford Cl COW/LTMR OX4 .... 51 E5
Radley Rd ABGD OX14 .... 68 B5
    ABGD OX14 .... 73 H1
Rahere Rd COW/LTMR OX4 ...... 51 H5
Railway La COW/LTMR OX4 .... 61 F1
Rainbow Wy ABGD OX14 .... 68 A3
Raleigh Park Rd
    OXN/BOT/CM OX2.............. 49 F1
Rampion Cl COW/LTMR OX4 .... 62 D1 🔟
Ramsey Rd HEAD OX3 .... 42 B2
Ramsons Wy ABGD OX14 .... 74 B1
Randolph St COW/LTMR OX4 ..... 51 E1
Rawlings Gv ABGD OX14 .... 73 E1
Rawlinson Rd OXN/BOT/CM OX2 .. 32 A5
Rawson Cl OXN/BOT/CM OX2 .... 31 G1
Raymund Rd HEAD OX3 .... 33 E5
Reade Av ABGD OX14 .... 74 A1
Recreation Rd WDSTK OX20....... 5 F3
Rectory La WDSTK OX20.......... 4 D3
Rectory Rd COW/LTMR OX4 .... 3 J7
Red Bridge Hollow OX/KTN OX1 ... 50 B4
Red Copse La OX/KTN OX1....... 59 H1

Rede Cl HEAD OX3 .... 42 B5
Redland Rd HEAD OX3 .... 33 G5
Red Lion Sq OX/KTN OX1 .... 2 C5 🔟
Redmoor Cl COW/LTMR OX4 ..... 61 H1
Redwood Cl COW/LTMR OX4 ..... 52 B1
Reedmace Cl COW/LTMR OX4 .. 62 D1 🔟
Regent St COW/LTMR OX4 .... 51 E1
Rest Harrow COW/LTMR OX4 ... 62 C1 🔟
Rewley Rd OXN/BOT/CM OX2 ..... 2 A5
Reynolds Wy ABGD OX14 .... 73 F4
Richards La OXN/BOT/CM OX2 ... 31 H3
Richards Wy HEAD OX3 .... 42 C3
Richmond Rd OXN/BOT/CM OX2.... 2 B4
Rickyard Cl OXN/BOT/CM OX2 .... 2 A4 🔟
Riddell Pl OXN/BOT/CM OX2 ..... 31 H1 🔟
Ridgefield Rd COW/LTMR OX4..... 51 F1
Ridgemont Cl
    OXN/BOT/CM OX2 .... 31 H3 🔟
Ridgeway Rd HEAD OX3 .... 42 C2
The Ridings HEAD OX3 .... 42 C5
    KID OX5 .... 13 E3
Ridley Rd COW/LTMR OX4 .... 52 B2
Riely Cl WIT/EY OX8 .... 9 H3
Riley Cl ABGD OX14 .... 73 E3
Rimmer Cl HEAD OX3 .... 33 E5
Ringwood Rd HEAD OX3 .... 42 D2
Rippington Ct ABGD OX14 .... 78 C2
Rippington Dr HEAD OX3 .... 41 E1
The Rise KID OX5 .... 14 D3
River Cl HEAD OX3 .... 34 B4
Rivermead Rd COW/LTMR OX4 ... 51 E5
Riverside Rd OXN/BOT/CM OX2 .. 39 G4
River Vw COW/LTMR OX4 .... 61 F4
    OX/KTN OX1.................. 60 D2
Rivy Cl ABGD OX14 .... 74 B1
Robert Robinson Av
    COW/LTMR OX4 .... 61 H2
Robsart Pl OXN/BOT/CM OX2 ... 47 H4 🔟
Rock Edge HEAD OX3 .... 42 A4
Rock Farm La COW/LTMR OX4 ... 61 G3
Rogers St OXN/BOT/CM OX2 ..... 32 A3
Rolfe Pl HEAD OX3 .... 41 F2
Roman Rd WHLY OX33 .... 54 D1
Roman Wy HEAD OX3 .... 25 E4
Rookery Cl MCHM/KBPZ OX13... 66 C5
The Rookery KID OX5 .... 13 E4 🔟
Roosevelt Dr HEAD OX3 .... 41 H4
Roosevelt Rd WIT/EY OX8 .... 9 G4
Rosamund Dr WDSTK OX20 .... 4 D2
Rosamund Rd OXN/BOT/CM OX2 .. 31 H2
Rose Av ABGD OX14 .... 67 G3
Rose Gdns OXN/BOT/CM OX2 .... 38 D5
Rose Hl COW/LTMR OX4 .... 51 G4 🔟
Rose La OX/KTN OX1 .... 3 F6
Rotha Field Rd
    OXN/BOT/CM OX2 .... 31 H3 🔟
Roundham Cl KID OX5 .... 13 E3 🔟
The Roundway HEAD OX3 ...... 42 C2 🔟
Routh Rd HEAD OX3 .... 42 C1
Rowan Cl KID OX5 .... 13 F5
Rowan Gv COW/LTMR OX4 ..... 62 D2 🔟
Rowel Dr KID OX5 .... 12 C3
Rowland Cl OXN/BOT/CM OX2... 31 E2
Row Leigh La MCHM/KBPZ OX13 .. 57 G5
Rowles Cl OX/KTN OX1 .... 60 D2
Rowney Pl COW/LTMR OX4 ...... 51 F4
Rupert Rd COW/LTMR OX4........ 52 B2
Rushmead Copse ABGD OX14 ... 68 B4 🔟
Ruskin Av ABGD OX14 .... 73 F4
Russell Jackson Cl WGFD OX10 ... 77 E3
Russell St OXN/BOT/CM OX2 .... 39 H4 🔟
Rutherford Cl ABGD OX14 .... 67 H5
Rutherway OXN/BOT/CM OX2..... 39 H1
Rutten La KID OX5 .... 20 B1
Rutters Cl KID OX5 .... 13 E4
Rymers La COW/LTMR OX4 ...... 51 G3

S

Sadlers Cft STAD OX44 .... 63 H2 🔟
Saffron Cl ABGD OX14 .... 74 A1 🔟
Sage Wk COW/LTMR OX4 .... 62 C2
St Amand Dr ABGD OX14 .... 73 F5
St Andrews Cl ABGD OX14 .... 68 B4
St Andrew's La HEAD OX3 .... 42 A1
St Andrew's Rd HEAD OX3 ...... 41 H1
St Anne's Rd HEAD OX3 .... 42 A3
St Barnabas St OXN/BOT/CM OX2 .. 2 A3
St Bernard's Rd OXN/BOT/CM OX2.. 2 A1
St Christopher's Pl
    COW/LTMR OX4 .... 51 H4 🔟
St Clement's St COW/LTMR OX4 ... 3 H6
St Cross Rd OX/KTN OX1.......... 2 F5
St Ebbes St OX/KTN OX1 .... 2 C6
St Edmund's La ABGD OX14 ..... 73 G3 🔟

St Edward's Av
    OXN/BOT/CM OX2.
St Giles KID OX5
    OX/KTN OX1
St Helen's Ct ABGD OX14
St Helen's Whf ABGD OX14
St James Rd ABGD OX14
St Johns Dr KID OX5
St John's Rd ABGD OX14
St John St OX/KTN OX1.
St Lawrence Rd OX/KTN OX1
St Leonard's Rd HEAD OX3.
St Luke's Rd COW/LTMR OX4.
St Margaret's Rd
    OXN/BOT/CM OX2.
St Martin's Rd COW/LTMR OX4
St Mary's Cl COW/LTMR OX4
    KID OX5
    WHLY OX33
St Mary's Gn ABGD OX14
St Mary's Rd COW/LTMR OX4
Saint Michael's Av ABGD OX14
St Michael's La KID OX5
St Michael's St OX/KTN OX1.
St Nicholas' Gn OXN/BOT/CM OX2
St Nicholas Rd COW/LTMR OX4.
St Omer Rd COW/LTMR OX4.
St Paul's Crs OXN/BOT/CM OX2.
St Peter's Cl MCHM/KBPZ OX13.
    WIT/EY OX8
St Peter's Rd ABGD OX14
    OXN/BOT/CM OX2.
St Swithun's Rd OX/KTN OX1.
St Thomas' St OX/KTN OX1
Salegate La COW/LTMR OX4
Salesian Gdns COW/LTMR OX4 ..
Salford Rd HEAD OX3
Salisbury Crs OXN/BOT/CM OX2 ..
Salter Cl OX/KTN OX1
Samphire Rd COW/LTMR OX4
Sandfield Rd HEAD OX3
Sandford Cl ABGD OX14
Sandford La OX/KTN OX1
Sandford Rd COW/LTMR OX4.
Sandhill Rd KID OX5.
Sand La HEAD OX3
Sandleigh Rd MCHM/KBPZ OX13
Sandy La COW/LTMR OX4.
    KID OX5
    OX/KTN OX1
Sandy La West COW/LTMR OX4.
Saunders Rd COW/LTMR OX4
Savile Rd OX/KTN OX1
Sawpit Rd COW/LTMR OX4
Saxifrage Sq COW/LTMR OX4 ..
Saxon Wy HEAD OX3
Saxton Rd ABGD OX14
Scholar Pl OXN/BOT/CM OX2
Schongau Cl ABGD OX14
School Ct OXN/BOT/CM OX2
School La ABGD OX14
School Pl OX/KTN OX1
School Rd KID OX5
Scott Cl KID OX5
Scott Rd OXN/BOT/CM OX2
Seacourt Rd OXN/BOT/CM OX2.
Sefton Rd HEAD OX3
Sellwood Rd ABGD OX14
Selwyn Crs ABGD OX14.
Sermon Cl HEAD OX3.
Seventh Av HEAD OX3
Severn Rd MCHM/KBPZ OX13
Sewell Cl ABGD OX14
Shadwell Rd WGFD OX10
Shaftsbury Rd HEAD OX3.
Shakespeare Rd WIT/EY OX8.
Shaw's Copse ABGD OX14
Sheepway Ct COW/LTMR OX4
Sheldon Wy COW/LTMR OX4
Shelford Pl HEAD OX3
Shelley Cl ABGD OX14
    HEAD OX3
Shelley Rd COW/LTMR OX4
Shepherd Gdns ABGD OX14
Shepherds Hl COW/LTMR OX4
Sheriff's Dr OXN/BOT/CM OX2 ..
Sherwood Av ABGD OX14
Ship St OX/KTN OX1.
Shipton Rd WDSTK OX20
Shire Lake Cl OX/KTN OX1
Shoe La OX/KTN OX1.
Shotover Kilns HEAD OX3.
Shrieves Cl ABGD OX14
Sidney St COW/LTMR OX4
Silkdale Cl COW/LTMR OX4
Silver Rd COW/LTMR OX4
Simon's Cl WHLY OX33
Simpsons Wy OX/KTN OX1

laas Cl ABGD OX14 ...... 73 E5 [1]
I HEAD OX3 ...... 42 A4
e HEAD OX3 ...... 42 A4
ker Cl HEAD OX3 ...... 42 C3 [2]
n Mede HEAD OX3 ...... 41 F1 [2]
s Cl OXN/BOT/CM OX2 ...... 48 C1
BOT/CM OX4 ...... 52 C5
Av ABGD OX14 ...... 67 H4
X5 ...... 21 F1
y Cl MCHM/KBPZ OX13 ...... 56 D3
I KID OX5 ...... 21 G2
roft HEAD OX3 ...... 33 E4
ale Rd OXN/BOT/CM OX2 ...... 32 A2
nd STAD OX44 ...... 63 H2
rn By-pass Rd
TN OX1 ...... 49 H2
BOT/CM OX2 ...... 39 E5
eld Rd COW/LTMR OX4 ...... 41 F5
noor Pl
BOT/CM OX2 ...... 40 A1 [2]
noor Rd
OX2 ...... 39 H2
noor Wy ABGD OX14 ...... 73 F1
Pde OXN/BOT/CM OX2 ...... 31 H4
Parks Rd OX/KTN OX1 ...... 2 E5
St OXN/BOT/CM OX2 ...... 39 H5
cre La WIT/EY OX8 ...... 28 A2
y Pl OXN/BOT/CM OX2 ...... 32 A1
ears KID OX5 ...... 20 C1
well St OX/KTN OX1 ...... 2 D7 [3]
er Av KID OX5 ...... 20 C2
er Crs COW/LTMR OX4 ...... 51 F4
ve Cl ABGD OX14 ...... 67 G4
d MCHM/KBPZ OX13 ...... 66 D3
eberry Cl
/LTMR ...... 62 B1 [1]
ers KID OX5 ...... 13 G3
y Fld COW/LTMR OX4 ...... 62 B2 [13]
nney ABGD OX14 ...... 67 E5
Ct HEAD OX3 ...... 42 B2
Copse OX/KTN OX1 ...... 50 B5
field Dr ABGD OX14 ...... 73 F1
Field Rd KID OX5 ...... 13 G4
BOT/CM OX2 ...... 38 D5 [1]
Gdns ABGD OX14 ...... 73 E2
Hill Rd KID OX5 ...... 12 A4
La COW/LTMR OX4 ...... 62 A1
OX3 ...... 42 C2
OX33 ...... 53 F1
Rd ABGD OX14 ...... 73 E2
Gdns COW/LTMR OX4 ...... 62 B3 [3]
R KID OX5 ...... 13 F5
ney La OXN/BOT/CM OX2 ...... 31 H2
Cl OXN/BOT/CM OX2 ...... 2 A5
er Pl HEAD OX3 ...... 41 E1
eld Rd HEAD OX3 ...... 33 G5 [4]
d Dr ABGD OX14 ...... 73 G2
y Cl OXN/BOT/CM OX2 ...... 39 E5
y Rd COW/LTMR OX4 ...... 51 E1
eld Pl HEAD OX3 ...... 42 B4 [2]
eld Cl HEAD OX3 ...... 42 C4
n Harcourt Rd
EY OX8 ...... 26 C5
n Rd OXN/BOT/CM OX2 ...... 49 F2
y OX33 ...... 35 H5
le Rd OXN/BOT/CM OX2 ...... 48 C1
ay Rd HEAD OX3 ...... 42 C2
con Rd HEAD OX3 ...... 41 H3
n Ap KID OX5 ...... 12 D2
d ABGD OX14 ...... 81 E1
...... 7 H1
OX33 ...... 44 B5
EY OX8 ...... 26 B5
EY OX8 ...... 28 B3
on Rd HEAD OX3 ...... 41 G2
ton Rd OXN/BOT/CM OX2 ...... 32 A5
HEAD OX3 ...... 33 H5
n Cl ABGD OX14 ...... 73 F4
en Rd HEAD OX3 ...... 41 H2
g Cl KID OX5 ...... 13 F4
g Rd KID OX5 ...... 13 F4
g Road Ap KID OX5 ...... 13 F3
d ABGD OX14 ...... 73 G2
...... 61 E4
ton Rd ABGD OX14 ...... 78 B4
rt St OX/KTN OX1 ...... 50 B2 [1]
d HEAD OX3 ...... 42 A2
sons Cl OXN/BOT/CM OX2 ...... 38 B4
ey End ABGD OX14 ...... 68 B4
eys Rd HEAD OX3 ...... 33 F5
Tree Cl KID OX5 ...... 20 C2 [2]
Pl HEAD OX3 ...... 41 H1
Cl KID OX5 ...... 38 C4
hill La ABGD OX14 ...... 72 D5
Quarry La
/LTMR ...... 51 F4 [3]

Stone St COW/LTMR OX4 ...... 41 F5
Stonhouse Crs ABGD OX14 ...... 68 D4
Stonor Pl HEAD OX3 ...... 41 G3
Stoutsfield Cl KID OX5 ...... 20 B2
Stowford Rd HEAD OX3 ...... 42 C1
Stowood Cl HEAD OX3 ...... 42 B1
Stratfield Rd KID OX5 ...... 21 F1
OXN/BOT/CM OX2 ...... 32 A3
Stratford Dr WIT/EY OX8 ...... 28 A2
Stratford St COW/LTMR OX4 ...... 50 D1
Stratton Wy ABGD OX14 ...... 73 G2
Stubble Cl OXN/BOT/CM OX2 ...... 38 B5 [2]
Stubbs Av HEAD OX3 ...... 52 B1
Sturges Cl HEAD OX3 ...... 42 B1 [3]
Suffolk Wy ABGD OX14 ...... 73 E3
Sugworth Crs ABGD OX14 ...... 60 D5 [1]
Sugworth La MCHM/KBPZ OX13 ...... 60 A5
Summerfield OX/KTN OX1 ...... 50 C2 [2]
Summerhill Rd
OXN/BOT/CM OX2 ...... 32 A3
Summertown Ct
OXN/BOT/CM OX2 ...... 31 H3 [2]
Sunderland Av OXN/BOT/CM OX2 ...... 31 H1
Sundew Cl COW/LTMR OX4 ...... 62 D1
Sunningwell Rd
MCHM/KBPZ OX13 ...... 59 G5
MCHM/KBPZ OX13
OX/KTN OX1 ...... 50 C3
Sunny Ri WHLY OX33 ...... 53 G2
Sunnyside COW/LTMR OX4 ...... 51 E2 [2]
WHLY OX33 ...... 44 D5 [2]
Sutton Cl ABGD OX14 ...... 73 G2
Sutton Rd HEAD OX3 ...... 33 G5
Sutton Wick La ABGD OX14 ...... 78 C2
Swallow Cl COW/LTMR OX4 ...... 62 C2 [13]
Swan La WIT/EY OX8 ...... 9 G3
Swan St OXN/BOT/CM OX2 ...... 39 H4
WIT/EY OX8 ...... 28 B3
Sweetmans Rd
OXN/BOT/CM OX2 ...... 49 E1
Swift Cl COW/LTMR OX4 ...... 62 C2
Swinbourne Rd COW/LTMR OX4 ...... 61 G1
Swinburne Rd ABGD OX14 ...... 73 H1
COW/LTMR 51 E2
Swinford Bridge (Toll)
WIT/EY OX8 ...... 28 D4
Sworford La WHLY OX33 ...... 55 G2
Sycamore Cl MCHM/KBPZ OX13 ...... 66 C5
Sycamore Crs OX/KTN OX1 ...... 60 D4
Sycamore Rd OXN/BOT/CM OX2 ...... 49 E1
Sympson Cl HEAD OX3 ...... 73 F3

T

Tackley Pl OXN/BOT/CM OX2 ...... 40 A1
Taggs Ga HEAD OX3 ...... 42 C1
Talbot Rd OXN/BOT/CM OX2 ...... 21 H5
Tanners La WIT/EY OX8 ...... 28 C3
Tarragon Dr COW/LTMR OX4 ...... 62 C2
Tatham Rd ABGD OX14 ...... 67 G5
Taverner Pl HEAD OX3 ...... 41 E1
Tawney St COW/LTMR OX4 ...... 41 F5
Teal Cl COW/LTMR OX4 ...... 62 C2 [13]
Templar Rd OXN/BOT/CM OX2 ...... 32 A1
Templars Wy WHLY OX33 ...... 44 B5 [2]
Temple Rd COW/LTMR OX4 ...... 51 H2
Temple St COW/LTMR OX4 ...... 40 D5
The Tennis WIT/EY OX8 ...... 19 F5
Tennyson Dr ABGD OX14 ...... 72 D4
Tern Wk COW/LTMR OX4 ...... 62 B2
Terrington Cl ABGD OX14 ...... 67 G4
Thackley End OXN/BOT/CM OX2 ...... 32 A5
Thame La ABGD OX14 ...... 74 B5
Thame Rd STAD OX44 ...... 65 G4
Thames Pth ABGD OX14 ...... 79 G2
OXN/BOT/CM OX2 ...... 30 C2
OXN/BOT/CM OX2 ...... 39 H3
WIT/EY OX8 ...... 30 A1
WIT/EY OX8 ...... 46 C5
Thames St ABGD OX14 ...... 73 G3
OX/KTN OX1 ...... 2 C7
OX/KTN OX1 ...... 40 B5
WIT/EY OX8 ...... 28 B3 [1]
Thames Vw ABGD OX14 ...... 73 H2
Thames View Rd COW/LTMR OX4 ...... 61 E1
Thesiger Rd ABGD OX14 ...... 73 G1
Third Acre Ri OXN/BOT/CM OX2 ...... 38 C5
Thistlecroft Cl ABGD OX14 ...... 68 A4 [7]
Thistle Dr COW/LTMR OX4 ...... 62 D1
Thomson Ter COW/LTMR OX4 ...... 61 F1
Thornbury Rd WIT/EY OX8 ...... 28 A3
Thorncliffe Rd OXN/BOT/CM OX2 ...... 32 A4
Thorne Cl KID OX5 ...... 12 D3
Thornhill Wk ABGD OX14 ...... 67 F5
Three Corners Rd
COW/LTMR OX4 ...... 62 D1

Three Fields Rd HEAD OX3 ...... 42 B5 [6]
Thrift Pl COW/LTMR OX4 ...... 62 C1 [3]
Thrupp La ABGD OX14 ...... 74 C1
Thrupp Rd ABGD OX14 ...... 68 D5
Thurston Rd ABGD OX14 ...... 73 F3
Tidmarsh La OX/KTN OX1 ...... 2 B6 [4]
Tilbury La OXN/BOT/CM OX2 ...... 38 D3
Tilehouse Cl HEAD OX3 ...... 42 B2 [6]
Tilgarsley Rd WIT/EY OX8 ...... 28 A2
Timothy Wy COW/LTMR OX4 ...... 62 C1 [6]
Titup Hall Dr HEAD OX3 ...... 42 B4
Tollgate Rd ABGD OX14 ...... 80 A2
Toot Hill Butts HEAD OX3 ...... 42 C2
Tower Cl ABGD OX14 ...... 73 E3
Tower Rd WGFD OX10 ...... 77 C3
Town Cl ABGD OX14 ...... 79 H5
Town Furlong MCHM/KBPZ OX13 ...... 56 D3
Town Furze HEAD OX3 ...... 52 A1
The Town Gn KID OX5 ...... 13 G3
Townsend ABGD OX14 ...... 73 G4
Townsend Sq COW/LTMR OX4 ...... 51 E2 [2]
Toynbee Cl OXN/BOT/CM OX2 ...... 49 E1
Trafford Rd HEAD OX3 ...... 42 B2
Tree Close Bay COW/LTMR OX4 ...... 51 F4 [2]
Treeground Pl KID OX5 ...... 13 F4
Tree La OXN/BOT/CM OX2 ...... 51 F4
Trefoil Pl COW/LTMR OX4 ...... 62 D1 [2]
Trevor Pl COW/LTMR OX4 ...... 51 E2
Trinity Cl ABGD OX14 ...... 68 A4
Trinity Rd HEAD OX3 ...... 52 B1
Troy Cl HEAD OX3 ...... 52 B1
Tucker Rd COW/LTMR OX4 ...... 52 B5
Tudor Ct OXN/BOT/CM OX2 ...... 38 B5
The Tuer WIT/EY OX8 ...... 28 B3 [4]
Tullis Cl ABGD OX14 ...... 79 G5
Tumbledown Hl
OXN/BOT/CM OX2 ...... 47 G2
Turberville Cl ABGD OX14 ...... 73 F3
Turl St OX/KTN OX1 ...... 2 D5 [2]
Turnagain La ABGD OX14 ...... 73 G3
Turn Again La OX/KTN OX1 ...... 2 C7 [8]
Turner Cl COW/LTMR OX4 ...... 52 A2
Turner Rd ABGD OX14 ...... 73 E4
Turners Cl ABGD OX14 ...... 69 E4
Turnpike Rd OXN/BOT/CM OX2 ...... 48 C2
Twelve Acre Dr ABGD OX14 ...... 68 A3
Tyndale Pl WHLY OX33 ...... 44 D5 [3]
Tyndale Rd COW/LTMR OX4 ...... 3 H7
Tyne Rd MCHM/KBPZ OX13 ...... 66 D3

U

Ulfgar Rd OXN/BOT/CM OX2 ...... 31 G2
Underhill Circ HEAD OX3 ...... 42 C1 [3]
Union St OX/KTN OX1 ...... 3 K7
WDSTK OX20 ...... 5 E3
Upland Park Rd
OXN/BOT/CM OX2 ...... 31 H2
Upper Brook Hl WDSTK OX20 ...... 5 E3 [6]
Upper Campsfield Rd KID OX5 ...... 5 H4
Upper Fisher Rw OX/KTN OX1 ...... 2 A2
Upper Rd OX/KTN OX1 ...... 60 C1
Upton Cl ABGD OX14 ...... 67 H5
COW/LTMR OX4 ...... 61 H1
Upway Rd HEAD OX3 ...... 33 G5

V

Valentia Cl KID OX5 ...... 7 G1
Valentia Rd HEAD OX3 ...... 41 G3
Valley Rd WHLY OX33 ...... 53 G2
Vanbrugh Cl WDSTK OX20 ...... 4 D2
Van-dieman's La
COW/LTMR OX4 ...... 51 H5 [1]
Venables Cl OXN/BOT/CM OX2 ...... 2 A2
Verbena Wy COW/LTMR OX4 ...... 62 B2 [14]
Vermont Dr WDSTK OX20 ...... 4 D2 [2]
Vernon Av OXN/BOT/CM OX2 ...... 49 F2
Vetch Pl COW/LTMR OX4 ...... 62 C1
Vicarage Cl COW/LTMR OX4 ...... 61 G1
Vicarage La OX/KTN OX1 ...... 50 B2 [2]
Vicarage Rd KID OX5 ...... 13 G3
OX/KTN OX1 ...... 50 B2
Victoria Ct OX/KTN OX1 ...... 2 C5 [5]
Victoria Rd ABGD OX14 ...... 73 E2
OXN/BOT/CM OX2 ...... 32 A2
Victor St OXN/BOT/CM OX2 ...... 2 A3
Villeboys Cl ABGD OX14 ...... 74 B1
Villiers La COW/LTMR OX4 ...... 51 F4
Vineyard ABGD OX14 ...... 73 G2
Violet Wy COW/LTMR OX4 ...... 62 D1
Virginia Wy ABGD OX14 ...... 73 E5

W

Walkers Cl WIT/EY OX8 ...... 17 F1
The Walk KID OX5 ...... 15 E3 [1]
Wallace Cl ABGD OX14 ...... 73 F4
Walton Crs OXN/BOT/CM OX2 ...... 2 B3
Walton La OX/KTN OX1 ...... 2 B3
Walton St OXN/BOT/CM OX2 ...... 2 A2
Walton Well Rd
OXN/BOT/CM OX2 ...... 39 H2
Warburg Crs COW/LTMR OX4 ...... 52 C5
Warnborough Rd
OXN/BOT/CM OX2 ...... 40 A1
Warneford La HEAD OX3 ...... 41 G4
Warneford Rd COW/LTMR OX4 ...... 41 F5
Warren Crs HEAD OX3 ...... 42 A4
The Warren ABGD OX14 ...... 74 A1
Warren Vw STAD OX44 ...... 65 G4 [2]
Warwick Cl ABGD OX14 ...... 73 H1
Warwick St COW/LTMR OX4 ...... 51 E1
Wastie's Orch WIT/EY OX8 ...... 9 G3
Water Eaton La KID OX5 ...... 13 H5
Water Eaton Rd
OXN/BOT/CM OX2 ...... 32 B2
Watermead KID OX5 ...... 13 H4
Watermill Wy HEAD OX3 ...... 42 D1
Watery La ABGD OX14 ...... 76 A5
Watlington Rd COW/LTMR OX4 ...... 52 C5
STAD OX44 ...... 63 E2
Watson Crs MCHM/KBPZ OX13 ...... 58 B4
Waverley Av KID OX5 ...... 13 H4
Waxes Cl ABGD OX14 ...... 68 B4
Wayfaring Cl COW/LTMR OX4 ...... 62 B3 [4]
Waynflete Rd HEAD OX3 ...... 42 C1
Webb's Cl OXN/BOT/CM OX2 ...... 31 E2
Webb's Wy KID OX5 ...... 13 G3
Websters Cl WIT/EY OX8 ...... 17 F1
Weirs La OX/KTN OX1 ...... 50 C3
Weldon Rd HEAD OX3 ...... 41 E1
Welford Gdns ABGD OX14 ...... 67 H4
Welland Cl MCHM/KBPZ OX13 ...... 66 D4
Wellesbourne Cl ABGD OX14 ...... 74 A1
Wellington Pl OX/KTN OX1 ...... 2 C4
Wellington Sq OX/KTN OX1 ...... 2 B3 [8]
Wellington St OXN/BOT/CM OX2 ...... 2 A3
Wentworth Rd
OXN/BOT/CM OX2 ...... 32 A2
Wesley Cl COW/LTMR OX4 ...... 62 B1
West Av ABGD OX14 ...... 67 H4
Westbury Crs COW/LTMR OX4 ...... 51 G4
West Cft WGFD OX10 ...... 77 E4
Western By-pass Rd
OXN/BOT/CM OX2 ...... 30 D3
Western Rd OX/KTN OX1 ...... 50 B1
Westfield Cl ABGD OX14 ...... 51 G2
Westfield Rd ABGD OX14 ...... 81 H5
WHLY OX33 ...... 44 B4
Westfields ABGD OX14 ...... 73 E1
Westlands Dr HEAD OX3 ...... 33 G5
Westland Wy WDSTK OX20 ...... 4 D2
Westminster Wy
OXN/BOT/CM OX2 ...... 39 E5
OXN/BOT/CM OX2 ...... 49 F1 [6]
Westrup Cl HEAD OX3 ...... 3 J1
West Saint Helen St ABGD OX14 ...... 73 G3
West St OX/KTN OX1 ...... 39 H4
West Wy OXN/BOT/CM OX2 ...... 38 D4
Wesy Quay ABGD OX14 ...... 73 G5
Weyland Rd HEAD OX3 ...... 42 B3
Wey Rd WGFD OX10 ...... 77 F4
Wharf Cl ABGD OX14 ...... 73 F3
Wharton Rd HEAD OX3 ...... 42 A2
Wheatcroft Cl ABGD OX14 ...... 67 H4 [3]
Wheatley Br WHLY OX33 ...... 55 F1
Wheatley Rd KID OX5 ...... 15 E4
STAD OX44 ...... 63 H1
WHLY OX33 ...... 44 A1
Whitecross MCHM/KBPZ OX13 ...... 66 D1
White Hill La OX/KTN OX1 ...... 58 B2
Whitehorns Wy ABGD OX14 ...... 78 B3
Whitehouse Cl
MCHM/KBPZ OX13 ...... 66 D5
Whitehouse Rd OX/KTN OX1 ...... 50 B1
Whitelock Rd ABGD OX14 ...... 67 G5
White Rd COW/LTMR OX4 ...... 52 B3
Whites Forge MCHM/KBPZ OX13 ...... 56 D3
White's La ABGD OX14 ...... 68 C3
White Wy KID OX5 ...... 13 F4
Whitson Pl COW/LTMR OX4 ...... 51 F1 [3]
Wick Cl ABGD OX14 ...... 68 B4
HEAD OX3 ...... 42 B1
Wilberforce St HEAD OX3 ...... 42 A3 [1]
Wilcote Rd HEAD OX3 ...... 42 C1
Wilcote Vw WIT/EY OX8 ...... 8 B5
Wildmoor Ga ABGD OX14 ...... 67 E5
Wilkins Rd COW/LTMR OX4 ...... 52 A3

William Kimber Crs *HEAD* OX3........ **42** B2
William Orchard CI *HEAD* OX3........ **41** H1
Williamson Wy *COW/LTMR* OX4.... **61** F1
William St *HEAD* OX3...................... **3** K2
Willow Brook *ABGD* OX14............ **73** E2
Willow CI *KID* OX5............................ **20** B1
   STAD OX44.................................. **63** F1
Willows Edge *WIT/EY* OX8............ **28** A3
Willow Tree CI *MCHM/KBPZ* OX13.. **66** D5
Willow Wy *ABGD* OX14.................. **60** D4
   KID OX5...................................... **12** B4
Wilmots *STAD* OX44........................ **62** D5
Wilsdon Wy *KID* OX5.............. **13** E3
Wilsham Rd *ABGD* OX14................ **73** G3
Wimblestraw Rd *WGFD* OX10........ **77** F4
Winchester Rd
   OXN/BOT/CM OX2...................... **40** A1
Windale Av *COW/LTMR* OX4.......... **62** B1
Windmill CI *WIT/EY* OX8................ **16** A2
Windmill Hts *WIT/EY* OX8.............. **16** A1
Windmill La *WHLY* OX33................ **54** A1
Windmill Rd *HEAD* OX3.................. **42** A3
   WIT/EY OX8................................ **16** A1
Windrush Rd *WGFD* OX10.............. **77** F5
Windrush Wy *ABGD* OX14.............. **68** A5

Windsor Crs *HEAD* OX3 .... **32** D5 ⬛
Windsor St *HEAD* OX3 .... **42** A3 ⬛
Wingate CI *COW/LTMR* OX4 .... **52** B5 ⬛
The Winnyards
   OXN/BOT/CM OX2...................... **47** H4
Winsmore La *ABGD* OX14............ **73** G2
Winston CI *KID* OX5 .... **13** F5 ⬛
Winterborne Rd *ABGD* OX14 .... **73** E2
Wise Av *KID* OX5.................... **13** E3
Withington Ct *ABGD* OX14............ **73** G2
Witney Rd *WIT/EY* OX8 .... **9** F3
   WIT/EY OX8 .... **28** A2
Wolsey Ct *KID* OX5........................ **11** H1
Wolsey Rd *OXN/BOT/CM* OX2 ...... **32** A1
Wolvercote Gn
   OXN/BOT/CM OX2...................... **31** F2
Woodbine PI *OX/KTN* OX1 .... **2** A6 ⬛
Woodcroft *OX/KTN* OX1 .... **60** D2
Wood Farm Rd *HEAD* OX3 .... **42** B5
Woodhouse Wy *COW/LTMR* OX4.. **51** F3
Woodlands *WIT/EY* OX8 .... **9** F5
Woodlands CI *HEAD* OX3 .... **41** G2
Woodlands Rd *HEAD* OX3 .... **41** G2
Woodley CI *ABGD* OX14 .... **67** G3

Woodpecker Gn
   COW/LTMR OX4 .... **62** C2 ⬛
Woodperry Rd *HEAD* OX3.............. **25** E5
Woodruff CI *COW/LTMR* OX4 ...... **62** C1 ⬛
Woodside *WIT/EY* OX8 .... **16** B1 ⬛
Woodstock CI *OXN/BOT/CM* OX2 .. **31** H2
Woodstock Rd *KID* OX5 .... **12** B4
   KID OX5...................................... **21** E3
   OXN/BOT/CM OX2...................... **21** F5
   OXN/BOT/CM OX2...................... **31** H3
   WDSTK OX20................................ **5** H5
Woodstock Rd West *KID* OX5 ...... **12** A3
Wootton Rd *MCHM/KBPZ* OX13 .... **67** E2
Worcester PI *OX/KTN* OX1 .... **2** B4
Worcester St *OX/KTN* OX1 .... **2** B5
Wordsworth Rd *ABGD* OX14 .... **73** E4
Wren CI *WHLY* OX33.................... **44** C5
Wren Rd *OXN/BOT/CM* OX2 .... **32** B2
Wrightson CI *WHLY* OX33 .... **53** F2
Wroslyn Rd *WIT/EY* OX8 .... **9** E4
   WIT/EY OX8 .... **17** F3
Wyatt Rd *OXN/BOT/CM* OX2 ...... **32** A1
Wychwood La *HEAD* OX3 .... **42** D3
Wykeham Crs *COW/LTMR* OX4 .. **51** G4 ⬛
Wylie CI *HEAD* OX3........................ **42** A5

Wynbush Rd *COW/LTMR* OX4 ...... **62** B1
Wyndham Wy *OXN/BOT/CM* OX2 .. **32** A1
Wyndyke Furlong *ABGD* OX14 ...... **73** E1
Wytham CI *WIT/EY* OX8................ **28** A3
Wytham St *OX/KTN* OX1.............. **2** A5
Wytham Vw *WIT/EY* OX8.............. **16** A1

Y

Yarnell's HI *OXN/BOT/CM* OX2...... **31** H3
Yarnell's Rd *OXN/BOT/CM* OX2...... **31** H3
Yarnton Ct *KID* OX5........................ **12** B4
Yarnton La *KID* OX5........................ **11** H1
Yarnton Rd *WIT/EY* OX8................ **16** A1
Yeats CI *COW/LTMR* OX4 .... **62** B1
Yeftly Dr *COW/LTMR* OX4.............. **51** G4
Yeld Hall Rd *ABGD* OX14.............. **73** E2
Yewtree Ms *ABGD* OX14................ **67** G5
York Av *HEAD* OX3........................ **42** A2
York PI *COW/LTMR* OX4................ **32** A1
York Rd *HEAD* OX3........................ **42** A2
Ypres Wy *ABGD* OX14.................... **73** E1

Index - featured places

Abacus College
   OX/KTN OX1 .... **2** C5
Abbey Chiropody Clinic
   ABGD OX14 .... **73** F2
Abbey Sports Centre
   WGFD OX10 .... **77** F4
ABC Cinemas
   OX/KTN OX1 .... **2** C5
Abingdon College
   ABGD OX14 .... **67** F5
Abingdon Museum
   ABGD OX14 .... **73** G2
Abingdon Rugby Football Club
   ABGD OX14 .... **73** F5
Abingdon School
   ABGD OX14 .... **73** F2
The Abingdon Surgery
   ABGD OX14 .... **73** G2
The Acland Hospital
   OXN/BOT/CM OX2 .... **2** C1
All Souls College
   OX/KTN OX1 .... **2** E5
Apollo Theatre
   OX/KTN OX1 .... **2** C5
Aquinas Tutorial College
   COW/LTMR OX4 .... **40** D5
Artworks School of
   Art & Design
   COW/LTMR OX4 .... **51** E1
Ashmolean Museum
   OX/KTN OX1 .... **2** C4
Balliol College
   OX/KTN OX1 .... **2** D5
Banbury Road Medical Centre
   OXN/BOT/CM OX2 .... **32** A4
Banbury Road North
   Sports Ground
   OXN/BOT/CM OX2 .... **21** H5
Bartholomew School
   WIT/EY OX8 .... **28** A2
Barton Village First School
   HEAD OX3 .... **34** B5
Bayswater Middle School
   HEAD OX3 .... **42** C2
Berinsfield Health Centre
   WGFD OX10 .... **77** E4
Berinsfield Primary School
   WGFD OX10 .... **77** F4
Bernwood First School
   HEAD OX3 .... **42** B1
Bessels Leigh School
   MCHM/KBPZ OX13 .... **57** F4
Blackbird Leys Health Centre
   COW/LTMR OX4 .... **62** B1
Blackbird Leys Leisure Centre
   COW/LTMR OX4 .... **62** B1
Blenheim Palace
   WDSTK OX20 .... **4** D4
Bodleian Library
   OX/KTN OX1 .... **2** D4
Botley County Primary School
   OXN/BOT/CM OX2 .... **39** E4
Botley Medical Centre
   OXN/BOT/CM OX2 .... **38** D4
Boundary Business Park
   STAD OX44 .... **54** A5

Brasenose College
   OX/KTN OX1 .... **2** E5
Brasenose College
   Sports Ground
   OX/KTN OX1 .... **50** C1
Buckland University College
   HEAD OX3 .... **41** F2
The Burton Taylor Theatre
   OX/KTN OX1 .... **2** B4
Bury Knowle Health Centre
   HEAD OX3 .... **42** A2
Business School
   OX/KTN OX1 .... **2** A5
Caldecott Primary School
   ABGD OX14 .... **73** E4
Cardinal Newman Middle School
   COW/LTMR OX4 .... **51** F2
Carswell CP School
   ABGD OX14 .... **73** F2
Chandlings Manor School
   MCHM/KBPZ OX13 .... **60** A4
Cheney School
   HEAD OX3 .... **41** G4
The Cherwell School
   OXN/BOT/CM OX2 .... **32** B4
Chiltern Business Centre
   COW/LTMR OX4 .... **52** B4
Christ Church Cathedral School
   OX/KTN OX1 .... **2** D7
Christ Church College
   OX/KTN OX1 .... **2** E7
Christchurch Sports Ground
   OX/KTN OX1 .... **40** D5
Christs Hospital
   ABGD OX14 .... **73** G2
Church Cowley St James School
   COW/LTMR OX4 .... **51** H4
Churchill Hospital
   HEAD OX3 .... **41** H4
Church of England
   Primary School
   WIT/EY OX8 .... **9** F5
Clarendon Centre
   OX/KTN OX1 .... **2** C5
Clifton Hampden C of E Primary
   School
   ABGD OX14 .... **75** H5
College Oak
   ABGD OX14 .... **68** A4
College of Further Education
   COW/LTMR OX4 .... **62** B1
Convent Senior School
   ABGD OX14 .... **73** H1
Corpus Christi College
   OX/KTN OX1 .... **2** E6
Cothill Old School
   MCHM/KBPZ OX13 .... **66** A2
The County Gallery
   WIT/EY OX8 .... **28** A3
County Hall
   OX/KTN OX1 .... **2** C6
County Trading Estate
   COW/LTMR OX4 .... **52** C4
Covered Market
   OX/KTN OX1 .... **2** D5

Crescent School
   OXN/BOT/CM OX2 .... **31** H3
Culham College Institute
   ABGD OX14 .... **73** G3
Culham Parochial
   Primary School
   ABGD OX14 .... **80** A1
Cumnor C of E Primary School
   OXN/BOT/CM OX2 .... **47** H3
Cutteslowe Primary School
   OXN/BOT/CM OX2 .... **32** B1
Donnington Middle School
   COW/LTMR OX4 .... **51** F3
Doverbroecks College
   OXN/BOT/CM OX2 .... **40** B1
Dragon School
   OXN/BOT/CM OX2 .... **40** B1
Drayton County Primary School
   ABGD OX14 .... **78** C2
Drayton Golf Club
   ABGD OX14 .... **78** C5
Dr Souths C of E Primary School
   KID OX5 .... **15** E3
Dry Sandford County
   Primary School
   MCHM/KBPZ OX13 .... **58** A5
Dunmore County Infant School
   ABGD OX14 .... **67** G5
East Oxford First School
   COW/LTMR OX4 .... **3** K7
Eaton Practice
   MCHM/KBPZ OX13 .... **47** E5
Edward Field Primary School
   KID OX5 .... **13** G5
Emmanuel Christian School
   COW/LTMR OX4 .... **61** G1
Exeter College
   OX/KTN OX1 .... **2** D5
Exeter College Sports Ground
   HEAD OX3 .... **40** D1
Eye Hospital Radcliffe Infirmary
   OXN/BOT/CM OX2 .... **2** B3
Eynsham County Primary School
   WIT/EY OX8 .... **28** C2
Eynsham Medical Centre
   WIT/EY OX8 .... **28** B3
Ferry Sports Centre
   OXN/BOT/CM OX2 .... **32** A4
Fire Station
   OX/KTN OX1 .... **2** A5
Fitzharrys County
   Secondary School
   ABGD OX14 .... **67** G5
Frideswide Middle School
   OXN/BOT/CM OX2 .... **32** B4
Garsington C of E
   Primary School
   STAD OX44 .... **63** G1
Garsington Sports Club
   STAD OX44 .... **64** A1
Gosford All Blacks Rugby
   Football Club
   KID OX5 .... **12** C2
Gosford Hill Medical Centre
   KID OX5 .... **13** G5
Gosford Hill School
   KID OX5 .... **13** G5

Green College
   OXN/BOT/CM OX2 .... **2** B3
Hanborough Business Park
   WIT/EY OX8 .... **14** B3
Harris Manchester College
   OX/KTN OX1 .... **2** D4
Headington County Secondary
   Modern School
   HEAD OX3 .... **42** A3
Headington Quarry School
   HEAD OX3 .... **42** C4
Headington School
   HEAD OX3 .... **42** A4
Hertford College
   OX/KTN OX1 .... **2** D5
Hertford College Sports Ground
   HEAD OX3 .... **42** B2
Hinksey Business Centre
   OXN/BOT/CM OX2 .... **40** B6
Hinksey Polls Swimming
   OX/KTN OX1 .... **2** A7
Hollow Way Medical Centre
   COW/LTMR OX4 .... **51** H1
Holywell Business Centre
   OXN/BOT/CM OX2 .... **40** A2
Horspath C of E Primary School
   WHLY OX33 .... **54** A4
Iffley Mead School
   COW/LTMR OX4 .... **51** H2
The Infirmary
   ABGD OX14 .... **73** G3
Institute of Virology &
   Environmental Microbiology
   OX/KTN OX1 .... **2** A2
Isis Business Centre
   COW/LTMR OX4 .... **52** C4
Isis Clinic
   COW/LTMR OX4 .... **51** F1
Isis Middle School
   COW/LTMR OX4 .... **51** G4
Jericho Health Centre
   OXN/BOT/CM OX2 .... **2** B3
Jesus College
   OX/KTN OX1 .... **2** D5
Jesus College Sports Ground
   COW/LTMR OX4 .... **40** D5
John Mason School
   ABGD OX14 .... **73** F2
John Radcliffe Hospital
   HEAD OX3 .... **41** H4
John Watson School
   WHLY OX33 .... **44** C5
Jordan Hill Business Park
   OXN/BOT/CM OX2 .... **32** B1
Keble College
   OX/KTN OX1 .... **2** C4
Kennington Health Centre
   OX/KTN OX1 .... **2** A7
Kidlington & Gosford
   Sports Centre
   KID OX5 .... **13** F5
Kidlington Health Centre
   KID OX5 .... **13** F5
Kidlington Parish Council
   KID OX5 .... **13** F5
Kingfisher School
   ABGD OX14 ....

r Special School
  OX14 .... 74 A1
hool Oxford
  LTMR OX4 .... 52 A2
d School
  OX14 .... 72 D1
First School
  OX4 .... 51 F2
ollege
  'N OX1 .... 3 F2
ollege
  'N OX1 .... 2 D5
ollege Sports Ground
  LTMR OX4 .... 51 G1
ton School
  OX44 .... 65 G5
rlong Medical Centre
  .... 67 H3
rlong Primary School
  .... 67 H3
nborough Surgery
  Y OX8 .... 9 G3
ichard School
  OX4 .... 61 G1
n College
  OX1 .... 3 G6
n College School
  LTMR OX4 .... 3 H7
n College
  Ground
  OX3 .... 3 J4
allery
  'N OX1 .... 3 F5
house Surgery
  OX14 .... 73 G2
or County
ary School
  'Y OX8 .... 9 G3
or Preparatory School
  M/KBPZ OX13 .... 66 D5
urgery
  OX3 .... 41 H2
d College
  'N OX1 .... 2 E3
n Health Centre
  OX14 .... 72 D3
'N OX1 .... 2 C5
ough College
  'N OX1 .... 2 D6
ough School
  'K OX20 .... 5 F3
aldon C of E
ary School
  OX44 .... 70 D2
Health Centre
  OX3 .... 33 F5
Middle School
  OX3 .... 32 D5
w Arnold
ty Secondary School
  OX2 .... 48 D1
College
  'N OX1 .... 3 F6
Ford School for Girls
  OX3 .... 41 F2
House Surgery
  OX33 .... 44 C5
of Modern Art
  'N OX1 .... 2 D6
of Oxford
  'N OX1 .... 2 D6
of the
ry of Science
  'N OX1 .... 2 D5
lege
  'N OX1 .... 2 E4
lege School
  'N OX1 .... 2 E3
ksey School
  'N OX1 .... 50 B2
rston School
  OX3 .... 33 F5
n House School
  OX2 .... 31 H3
ld School
  LTMR OX4 .... 62 A2
nksey C of E School
  BOT/CM OX2 .... 39 F5
dlington School
  'K5 .... 13 F3
igh C of E School
  'Y OX8 .... 16 A1
igh Football Club
  'Y OX8 .... 16 C1
xford Medical Centre
  BOT/CM OX2 .... 32 A5

Northway Health Centre
  HEAD OX3 .... 33 G5
Northway Sports Centre
  HEAD OX3 .... 33 F5
Nuffield College
  OX/KTN OX1 .... 2 B5
Nuffield Hospital Management
  Committee
  HEAD OX3 .... 41 H4
Nuffield Industrial Estate
  COW/LTMR OX4 .... 61 H1
Oakfield Industrial Estate
  WIT/EY OX8 .... 28 A5
Old Fire Station Theatre
  OX/KTN OX1 .... 2 B5
The Old Gaol Leisure Centre
  ABGD OX14 .... 73 G3
The Open University
  OX/KTN OX1 .... 59 E2
Oriel College
  OX/KTN OX1 .... 2 E6
Oriel College Sports Ground
  COW/LTMR OX4 .... 41 G5
Ormerod School
  HEAD OX3 .... 42 D2
Osney Mead Industrial Estate
  OXN/BOT/CM OX2 .... 39 H5
Our Ladys RC School
  COW/LTMR OX4 .... 51 H3
Oxford Brookes University
  HEAD OX3 .... 41 F3
Oxford Brookes University
  WHLY OX33 .... 45 E4
Oxford Business Centre
  OX/KTN OX1 .... 2 A7
Oxford Bus Museum Trust
  WIT/EY OX8 .... 10 B3
Oxford City Council
  COW/LTMR OX4 .... 51 F5
Oxford City Council
  COW/LTMR OX4 .... 51 H2
Oxford City Council
  OX/KTN OX1 .... 2 C6
Oxford City Council
  OX/KTN OX1 .... 40 B5
Oxford City Council
  OX/KTN OX1 .... 50 C2
Oxford City Council
  OXN/BOT/CM OX2 .... 22 B5
Oxford City Football Club
  HEAD OX3 .... 33 F5
Oxford College of
  Further Education
  OX/KTN OX1 .... 2 B6
Oxford Community
  Health NHS Trust
  COW/LTMR OX4 .... 51 F3
Oxford Crown & County Court
  OX/KTN OX1 .... 40 B5
Oxford Gallery
  OX/KTN OX1 .... 2 E6
Oxford High School for Girls
  OXN/BOT/CM OX2 .... 32 B4
Oxford Ice Rink
  OX/KTN OX1 .... 2 B7
Oxford Marathon Rugby Club
  COW/LTMR OX4 .... 52 D2
Oxford Old Boys Rugby
  Football Club
  OXN/BOT/CM OX2 .... 32 B4
The Oxford Playhouse Theatre
  OX/KTN OX1 .... 2 C5
Oxford Radcliffe Hospital
  HEAD OX3 .... 41 H2
Oxford Regional Health
  Authority
  COW/LTMR OX4 .... 52 B5
Oxford Retail Park
  COW/LTMR OX4 .... 52 B5
Oxford Rugby Football Club
  OXN/BOT/CM OX2 .... 49 G1
Oxford School
  COW/LTMR OX4 .... 51 G1
Oxfordshire Community
  Health NHS Trust
  ABGD OX14 .... 72 D2
Oxfordshire Community
  Health NHS Trust
  COW/LTMR OX4 .... 41 F5
Oxfordshire County Council
  ABGD OX14 .... 73 F3
Oxfordshire County Council
  COW/LTMR OX4 .... 41 E5
Oxfordshire County Council
  COW/LTMR OX4 .... 52 B2
Oxfordshire County Council
  HEAD OX3 .... 42 A4

Oxfordshire County Council
  KID OX5 .... 12 D2
Oxfordshire County Council
  KID OX5 .... 20 B2
Oxfordshire County Council
  OX/KTN OX1 .... 2 B6
Oxfordshire County Museum
  WDSTK OX20 .... 4 D3
Oxfordshire Health Authority
  ABGD OX14 .... 73 F2
Oxfordshire Health Authority
  HEAD OX3 .... 41 H4
Oxfordshire Mental
  Healthcare NHS Trust
  COW/LTMR OX4 .... 41 H5
Oxfordshire Mental
  Healthcare NHS Trust
  COW/LTMR OX4 .... 61 G2
Oxford Spires Business Park
  KID OX5 .... 12 C1
Oxford Story
  OX/KTN OX1 .... 2 C5
Oxford Tutorial College
  OX/KTN OX1 .... 2 D6
Oxford United Football Club
  HEAD OX3 .... 41 H2
Oxford University Press
  OXN/BOT/CM OX2 .... 2 B3
Oxford University Rugby
  Football Club
  OX/KTN OX1 .... 50 D1
Paradise Street Business Centre
  OX/KTN OX1 .... 2 B6
Park Hospital for Children
  HEAD OX3 .... 41 H4
The Park Sports Centre
  WHLY OX33 .... 44 C4
Peachcroft Shopping Centre
  ABGD OX14 .... 68 A4
Pegasus First School
  COW/LTMR OX4 .... 62 C1
Pembroke College
  OX/KTN OX1 .... 2 C7
Pendon Museum
  ABGD OX14 .... 81 H5
Plater College
  ABGD OX14 .... 41 G3
Pusey House
  OX/KTN OX1 .... 2 C4
Quarry Surgery
  HEAD OX3 .... 42 A2
Queens College
  OX/KTN OX1 .... 3 F5
Queens College
  OXN/BOT/CM OX2 .... 32 B5
Queens College
  STAD OX44 .... 70 D3
Queens College Sports Ground
  OX/KTN OX1 .... 50 C1
Radcliffe Camera
  OX/KTN OX1 .... 2 E5
Radcliffe Infirmary NHS Trust
  OXN/BOT/CM OX2 .... 2 B2
Radley C of E Primary School
  ABGD OX14 .... 68 D3
Radley College
  ABGD OX14 .... 68 C2
Regents Park College
  OX/KTN OX1 .... 2 C4
Rhodes House
  OX/KTN OX1 .... 2 D3
Rose Hill Primary School
  COW/LTMR OX4 .... 51 F5
Rush Common County
  Primary School
  ABGD OX14 .... 68 A5
Ruskin College
  OX/KTN OX1 .... 2 B4
Rye St Antony School
  HEAD OX3 .... 41 G2
St Aldates College
  OX/KTN OX1 .... 2 C7
St Aloysius First School
  OXN/BOT/CM OX2 .... 40 A1
St Andrews C of E School
  HEAD OX3 .... 42 A2
St Annes College
  OXN/BOT/CM OX2 .... 2 C1
St Antonys College
  OXN/BOT/CM OX2 .... 2 B1
St Augustine of
  Canterbury School
  COW/LTMR OX4 .... 51 E3
St Barnabas C of E First School
  OX/KTN OX1 .... 2 A3
St Catherines College
  OX/KTN OX1 .... 3 H4

St Claires College
  OXN/BOT/CM OX2 .... 32 A5
St Clements Surgery
  COW/LTMR OX4 .... 40 D5
St Ebbes C of E First School
  OX/KTN OX1 .... 50 A1
St Edmunds Hall
  .... 3 F5
St Edmunds RC Primary School
  ABGD OX14 .... 73 H1
St Edwards School
  OXN/BOT/CM OX2 .... 32 A4
St Francis C E First School
  COW/LTMR OX4 .... 52 B2
St Hildas College
  OX/KTN OX1 .... 3 G7
St Hughes College
  OXN/BOT/CM OX2 .... 40 A1
St John Fisher School
  COW/LTMR OX4 .... 52 A5
St Johns College
  OX/KTN OX1 .... 2 D4
St Josephs RC School
  HEAD OX3 .... 41 F1
St Mary & St. John
  Primary School
  COW/LTMR OX4 .... 51 F1
St Michaels C of E First School
  HEAD OX3 .... 3 K3
St Nicholas First School
  HEAD OX3 .... 33 E5
St Nicolas C of E Primary School
  ABGD OX14 .... 73 G1
St Peters C of E School
  WIT/EY OX8 .... 19 F5
St Peters College
  OX/KTN OX1 .... 2 C5
St Philip & St. James
  Primary School
  OXN/BOT/CM OX2 .... 2 A1
St Swithuns C of E
  Primary School
  OX/KTN OX1 .... 60 D2
St Thomas More RC School
  KID OX5 .... 13 F5
Sandhills County
  Primary School
  HEAD OX3 .... 43 E1
School of St Helen &
  St. Katherine
  ABGD OX14 .... 73 E1
Scotts House School
  WIT/EY OX8 .... 16 C2
Sheldonian Theatre
  OX/KTN OX1 .... 2 E5
Somerville College
  OXN/BOT/CM OX2 .... 2 B2
South Oxford Health Centre
  OX/KTN OX1 .... 50 B2
Speedwell First School
  COW/LTMR OX4 .... 61 G1
Stanford House School
  OX/KTN OX1 .... 3 F6
The State of Space Theatre Co
  OXN/BOT/CM OX2 .... 32 A3
Summer Fields School
  OXN/BOT/CM OX2 .... 32 B3
Summertown Clinic
  OXN/BOT/CM OX2 .... 32 A2
Summertown Health Centre
  OXN/BOT/CM OX2 .... 32 A4
Sunningwell C of E School
  MCHM/KBPZ OX13 .... 59 F5
Sunningwell School of Art
  MCHM/KBPZ OX13 .... 59 G5
Temple Cowley County
  Middle School
  COW/LTMR OX4 .... 51 H2
Temple Cowley Health Centre
  COW/LTMR OX4 .... 52 A3
Temple Cowley Swimming Bath
  COW/LTMR OX4 .... 51 H3
Templeton College
  OX/KTN OX1 .... 50 C5
Thameside Primary School
  ABGD OX14 .... 73 E4
Thames View Business Centre
  ABGD OX14 .... 73 H2
Therapy Clinic
  WHLY OX33 .... 44 B5
Thomas Reade County
  Primary School
  ABGD OX14 .... 74 A1
Training Standards Council
  COW/LTMR OX4 .... 52 A4
Trinity College
  OX/KTN OX1 .... 2 D4